Milestones in Humanitarian Action

Milestones
in Humanitarian Action

Edited by Kevin M. Cahill, M.D.

The Center for International Humanitarian Cooperation
Fordham University Press IHA Book Series, New York, 2017

IHA Book Series

The International Humanitarian Affairs (IHA) Book Series, authored or edited by Kevin M. Cahill, M.D., is devoted to improving the effectiveness of humanitarian relief programs. With contributions by leading professionals, the books are practical guides to responding to the many different effects of civil strife, natural disasters, epidemics, and other crises. All books are available online at www.fordhampress.com. Books marked with an asterisk are available in French translation from Robert Laffont of Paris; books marked with a double asterisk are available in Spanish, German, Arabic, and French.

Preventive Diplomacy: Stopping Wars Before They Start, 1996, 2000*
Basics of International Humanitarian Missions, 2003*
Emergency Relief Operations, 2003*
Traditions, Values, and Humanitarian Action, 2003*
Human Security for All: A Tribute to Sérgio Vieira de Mello, 2004
Technology for Humanitarian Action, 2004
To Bear Witness: A Journey of Healing and Solidarity, 2005*
Tropical Medicine: A Clinical Text, 7th edition, 2006
The Pulse of Humanitarian Assistance, 2007
Even in Chaos: Education in Times of Emergency, 2010
Sudan at the Brink: Self-Determination and National Unity, F.D. Deng, Foreword by Kevin M. Cahill, M.D. 2010**
Tropical Medicine: A Clinical Text, 8th edition (Jubilee Edition), 2011**
More with Less: Disasters in an Era of Diminishing Resources, 2012
History and Hope: The International Humanitarian Reader, 2013
To Bear Witness: A Journey of Healing and Solidarity, 2nd expanded edition, 2013*
The Open Door: Art and Foreign Policy at the RCSI, 2014
An Unfinished Tapestry, 2015
A Dream for Dublin, 2016

IIHA Occasional Papers

Kevin M. Cahill, M.D., Abdulrahim Abby Farah, Abdirazak Haji Hussein, and David Shinn, The Future of Somalia: Stateless and Tragic, 2004
Mark Malloch Brown, International Diploma in Humanitarian Assistance, 2004
Francis Deng, Sudan: From Genocidal Wars to Frontiers of Peace and Unity, 2004
Kevin M. Cahill, M.D., The University and Humanitarian Action, 2008
Kevin M. Cahill, M.D., Romance and Reality in Humanitarian Action, 2008
Kevin M. Cahill, M.D., Gaza: Destruction and Hope, 2009
Daithi O'Ceallaigh, The Tale Towards a Treaty—A Ban on Cluster Munitions, 2010

Acronyms and Abbreviations

AUSMAT	Australian Medical Assistance Teams
CFR	Council on Foreign Relations (New York)
CIHC	Center for International Humanitarian Cooperation
CUNY	City University of New York
DARPA	Defense Advanced Research Policy Agency
EU	European Union
FU	Fordham University
FUP	Fordham University Press
GSAS	Graduate School of Arts and Sciences (Fordham University)
ICRC	International Committee of the Red Cross
IDHA	International Diploma in Humanitarian Assistance (Fordham University)
IDHL	International Diploma in Humanitarian Leadership (Fordham University)
IDMA	International Diploma in the Management of Humanitarian Action (Fordham University)
IDOHA	International Diploma in Operational Humanitarian Assistance (Fordham University)
IDP	Internally displaced person
IFRC	International Federation of Red Cross and Red Crescent Societies
IGO	Intergovernmental Organization
IHA	International Humanitarian Affairs
IIHA	Institute of International Humanitarian Affairs (Fordham University)
IMC	International Medical Corps
IOM	International Organization for Migration
ISAF	International Security Assistance Force
JRS	Jesuit Refugee Service
JUHAN	Jesuit University Humanitarian Action Network
MHCE	Mental Health in Conflict and Emergencies
mhGAP	Mental Health Gap Action Programme (WHO)
MIHA	Master of Arts in International Humanitarian Action (Fordham University)
MOU	Memorandum of Understanding
MSF	Médecins Sans Frontières
NGO	Non-Governmental Organization
NOHA	Network on Humanitarian Action

PGA	President of the UN General Assembly
RCSI	The Royal College of Surgeons in Ireland
UN	United Nations
UNAOC	United Nations Alliance of Civilizations
UNDHA	United Nations Department of Humanitarian Affairs
UNGA	United Nations General Assembly
UNHCR	United Nations High Commissioner for Refugees
UNICEF	United Nations Children's Fund
UNOCHA	United Nations Office for the Coordination of Humanitarian Affairs
UNRWA	United Nations Relief and Works Agency
WASH	Water, sanitation, and hygiene
WFP	World Food Programme
WHO	World Health Organization

For the IDHA tutors whose personal and practical field experiences have shaped our unique method of teaching.

Table of Contents

Acknowledgements

Over the past quarter century, many, many friends and colleagues have helped translate our early attempts to deal with complex humanitarian crises into practical training programs and an educational book series; some are mentioned by name in this volume, while others know of my gratitude for their advice, guidance, and loyal friendship. I have dedicated previous books to some, and noted others in earlier acknowledgments, in the body of texts, or in formal lectures.

For *Milestones in Humanitarian Action*, I thank my son, Denis Cahill, and Ms. Sarah Harper for editorial suggestions and, as importantly, for converting my handwritten thoughts, with multiple marginal corrections, into an acceptable style for the now necessary computer format. Mauro Sarri has once again been an essential part of the production and designed the book jacket.

Introduction

Pilgrims on spiritual journeys often mark their progress by pausing at special milestones along the path; they reflect on why and how they had come so far, and on plans for onward travel.

So, too, in the struggles of life are natural markers that encourage us to assess our original goals, to review accomplishments or failures, to recall important initiatives and personnel, to ultimately create our own milestones.

This book is a celebratory history, marking 25 years since the founding of the Center for International Humanitarian Cooperation (CIHC); the completion of 50 of our premier training course, the highly intensive, month-long International Diploma in Humanitarian Assistance (IDHA); the offering of dozens of other specialized courses; the publication of books, conference proceedings, and Occasional Papers, many translated into other languages and used in academic centers all over the world; the development of a Master of Arts in International Humanitarian Action (MIHA); the creation of an undergraduate Major in Humanitarian Studies, one of only four such programs offered in any university anywhere; and the establishment of an independent Institute of Humanitarian Affairs (IIHA) at Fordham University in New York. The IIHA coordinates these many global activities, and provides the legitimacy and credibility that can only be conferred by the degrees and diplomas offered by a university.

These are but some of the milestones we commemorate here, so that future generations entering the evolving profession of humanitarian assistance might appreciate the challenges faced by earlier pilgrims on a journey that embraced the spiritual as well as the practical elements of this noble, multidimensional discipline.

Beginnings

The CIHC was conceived, almost by accident, in the front room of my medical office in 1992, as the offspring of a casual comment by a dear friend and patient, Cyrus Vance, often regarded as the most respected American public servant of the twentieth century.

When I asked him about the worst obstacles he faced in the former Yugoslavia as the United Nations (UN) Special Representative of the Secretary-General, Cy said, "Non-governmental organizations (NGOs) and humanitarian workers who don't know what they're doing. They are often poorly trained and uncoordinated, causing endless and un-necessary problems."

That was, at least to me, a remarkable response, and led me down a path of inquiry and exploration. Mr. Vance's unexpected observation blossomed into a functioning CIHC, which over the past quarter century has trained thousands of relief workers from over 135 countries; helped to establish standards for the emerging discipline of international humanitarian assistance; and promoted a respect for, and understanding of, the importance of the practical details needed in responding to complex emergencies, while also meeting the highest demands of academia. Our publications are now used in universities and programs around the world.

The front conference room in my medical office in New York has served as the CIHC headquarters and home base since our founding. On the outside wall of that office, there is a bronze sign emblazoned with the CIHC logo: a pair of helping hands forming the dove of peace and encircling a central globe (image above).

An 18-year-old girl designed the logo, which captures, very beautifully, the essence and purpose of our mission.

A year after we opened our doors, at the first CIHC major conference, Cy noted, "It is only in the last year or so that I have come to understand the importance of health issues in world affairs. The CIHC—an important new organization, and the vision, dedication, and drive of my friend, Dr. Kevin Cahill—have informed us all about ways that government, private groups, and international organizations can begin to care for the health and well-being of all."

This focus on multilateral humanitarian activities was a dramatic departure for a US Secretary of State whose career had been dominated by Cold War politics and realities. We were off to a strong start.

Founding Board Members

The original dreams of the CIHC, the process of conception, and the early activities were based on the unique experiences of a close-knit, though widely diverse, Board of Directors, who defined startup programs and encouraged a flexibility necessary for the new organization to prosper.

Selecting a mutually supportive and active Board of Directors, who accept a common goal and are willing to give independent guidance, is an essential foundation for good management. The initial Board of the CIHC reflected the breadth of our goals, and offered the wisdom, perspective, and maturity required to navigate the destructive infighting that too often characterizes new projects, even in the supposedly altruistic world of charities established to offer assistance to those in need. Competition for funds and publicity, and the internecine, usually self-destructive battles of local politics, frequently dominate the agendas of non-governmental, governmental, and international organizations, overshadowing their capacity to provide desperately needed relief, and proper training for those privileged to share in life and death struggles on a grand scale.

The Founding Directors were persons with illustrious, international reputations in their own fields; they were confident, but not arrogant, and deeply concerned with the plight of the disadvantaged around the world. I knew each of them extremely well as their physician, and they were always available to me for consultations, meetings, and participation in field operations and training programs. Directors receive no salaries or any financial benefits from the CIHC. The biographical information on the Founding Members of the Board of Directors is listed below. I have served as the President of the CIHC since its inception, and therefore provide a brief outline of my own professional career in the About the Author section (page 181). Throughout the book, I will introduce subsequent Directors of the CIHC.

Cyrus Vance (1917–2002) had a remarkable career in public service for over 50 years. He variously served as the US Secretary of State, the Secretary of the Army, and the Deputy Secretary of Defense. I first worked with Cy in 1977, while I assisted the Somali government on issues of health in the context of the Ogaden War. I was struck by his intelligence, integrity, courage and loyalty—an opinion that never wavered. In the early 1990s, in response to the dissolution of Yugoslavia, Cy served as Special Envoy of the UN Secretary-General and did his part to build peace in that troubled region.

John Cardinal O'Connor (1920–2000) was the Catholic Archbishop of New York when he joined the Board of the CIHC. He previously served in the US Navy for 27 years, often entering combat zones in order to say Mass, and administer last rites to sailors and marines. He retired as Chief Chaplain with the rank of Rear Admiral. Cardinal O'Connor provided both a military and spiritual perspective to our deliberations, and generously donated half of his Navy pension to support our programs.

Paul Hamlyn (1926-2001) was a legendary publisher and philanthropist. He was also my closest adult friend, and a person whose quiet wisdom and counsel I could always rely upon. Paul shared with the CIHC his passionate interest in creating practical solutions for seemingly intractable problems. He generously supported many of our efforts to alleviate suffering and combat injustice. Despite progressive Parkinson's disease, he relished dangerous travels with me, whether to the war-torn Somali border or the hills of Nicaragua during the Contra War. He was awarded the Order of the British Empire in 1993 and appointed a British Life Peer in 1998.

Daniel Boyer was President of the American College in Switzerland; he acted as the CIHC Geneva Representative for many years, and was active on our behalf in various prisoner exchange programs in the former Yugoslavia.

Lord David Owen joined as a Director soon after the CIHC's incorporation as a public charity, and has served as Secretary of the Board since then. He previously worked as the UK Minister of the Navy, Minister of Health, and Foreign Minister. He first joined the Board while stationed as the European Union (EU) peace negotiator in the former Yugoslavia, where he worked with Cy Vance. Prior to his distinguished political career, David was a neurologist, and he has always brought a unique clinical and analytic perspective to the Board's deliberations. He has lectured on almost all of the 50 IDHA courses, and has been generous in sharing his time and wisdom with both faculty and students. He has been a major donor to CIHC projects.

Boutros Boutros-Ghali (1922–2016) was the sixth Secretary-General of the UN. He previously served for more than a decade as Egypt's Minister of State for Foreign Affairs. In the last chapter of this book, Preventive Diplomacy (page 157), I return to an early CIHC milestone, and pay tribute to this remarkable man.

Early Years (1992-1997)

Throughout the early years, the Directors carefully considered the best approach for the CIHC to adopt in order to make a unique contribution in international humanitarian affairs. At the time, academia had developed little in the way of practical courses to address the multiple dimensions of complex humanitarian crises. We consulted widely with those responsible for the medical, public health, logistical, legal, security, shelter, sanitation, food, and educational needs of people caught in the aftermath of natural disasters or conflicts, and began to construct a curriculum to implement our approach.

Humanitarian crises demand many different skills, and an effective response has different goals than those I had honed in tropical medicine, my professional area of expertise. The curing of illnesses, and even the eradication of diseases, are the aims in medical practice, whereas containment and relief are the more realistic goals in a humanitarian response. An emphasis must be placed on early warning systems, preparedness, coordination of international, state and private providers, regional stockpiling of supplies, the use of a cluster system in response, and appropriate lines for decisions that will often require unusual levels of military-civilian cooperation.

The CIHC developed programs in which students learn the practical and technical components of humanitarian aid from teachers with extensive field experience. Our main training courses are residential in order to simulate the long hours and close quarters that one experiences in disaster zones and refugee camps. Our teaching programs satisfy the highest academic standards, with all diplomas and degrees conferred by Fordham University, and we have not compromised on oral and written exams, research papers, and presentations.

Our other, equally important, focus has been the publication of books, conference reports, and Occasional Papers to complement the lectures and field exercises provided in a university setting. The CIHC has co-published, and owns the copyright to, 15 books on various aspects of humanitarian affairs; all royalties from these books go toward our student scholarship fund.

The CIHC is founded on a number of fundamental beliefs that have guided our actions over the past quarter of a century. These include:

1. That the CIHC be established as a public, as opposed to a private, charity under New York State laws, and meet the strictest auditing standards for transparency and record keeping for all income and expenses.

2. That the CIHC select and fund a minimal staff, including a lead teacher, an administrator, and tutors. As noted earlier, none of the Directors receive salaries or any financial benefits for their services.

3. That all teaching material, both in the classroom and in our publications, reflects the importance of practical field oriented experiences.

4. That our academic degrees, diplomas, and certificates permit students to move between humanitarian agencies and organizations throughout the world, with the hope that employers increasingly recognize and require accepted training standards.

5. That we attract a diverse and global student body, with particular emphasis on candidates from developing nations with limited access to internationally recognized courses. Because scholarship funds are an essential component of the program, the CIHC has strived to keep administrative costs to a minimum. All lecturers and authors are asked to donate their services, and one of my primary duties, as President, is to raise funds. Happily, over the last 25 years, the CIHC has secured over $6 million in charitable gifts and grants.

6. That the CIHC aim not only to emphasize training in international humanitarian affairs, including core curricula for all field workers from the many disciplines involved in handling complex emergencies, but also to actively participate in field operations when circumstances and contacts allow. In the early years, projects in Somalia and the former Yugoslavia dominated our institutional activities. Over the next 15 years, the CIHC provided funds for our Humanitarian Course Director, Larry Hollingworth, to assist UN operations in conflict zones at a senior level. I have served as the Chief Advisor on Humanitarian and Public Health Issues for three Presidents of the United Nations General Assembly (PGA). I maintained medical, research, and relief operations in Africa and Central America, and in my UN capacity, I accompanied the PGA and the UN Secretary-General on formal visits to Somalia, and to refugee camps around the world. Other CIHC field efforts are detailed below.

I.   Field Efforts

The crises in the former Yugoslavia and Somalia, two of the first faced by the humanitarian world after the collapse of the Soviet Union, presented the CIHC with challenges as to how, despite our limited budget, we could assist with concrete, practical relief programs. In many ways, these early efforts tested our ability to offer alternative approaches to complex humanitarian crises, expanded the reach of our Board Members' reputations and contacts, and set a strong precedent for future interventions and initiatives.

Somali-Lifeline (1992)

In the early 1990s, the government of Somalia collapsed, and the situation demanded competent professionals who could lead massive relief efforts. Yet the UN and major international NGOs seemed to consistently select humanitarian leaders from the Western world, most of whom were ignorant of Somalia's languages, cultures, and clan structure. The CIHC Board believed we could provide an alternative.

I had worked in Somalia since the early 1960s, and felt I knew the country and the people well. Many Somali professionals who lived outside the country's borders remained underutilized in the ongoing relief efforts. The CIHC believed that a directory of these professionals would allow players in the international community to better identify Somali nationals with expertise in a variety of humanitarian disciplines, who would then be in a position to stay and help the country rebuild after the conflict.

Two remarkable Somali leaders, Abdulrahim Abby Farah and Abdirizak Haji Hussein, assisted me in this effort. Abdulrahim previously served as both the UN Permanent Representative for Somalia and later as UN Under-Secretary-General for Special Political Affairs. I first met him in 1962 in Somalia, while he was a government official in the newly independent nation, and I was conducting research on epidemic diseases in the region. We remained close throughout his extensive diplomatic career and traveled together on several missions to troubled areas of Africa.

Abdirizak, often referred to as the "George Washington of Somalia," served as the country's Prime Minister from 1964 to 1969. In the aftermath of the 1969 military coup, he was imprisoned and placed in solitary confinement. In 1973, his captors took him from his cell and brought him to where he believed would be his place of execution. Instead he boarded a plane to New York, where he was welcomed as the newest Somali Ambassador to the UN—a strange turn of events that partially sums up the peculiarities of both Somali and UN politics. He sought political asylum several years later, and worked as a health expert within an office I then directed in New York State.

We soon developed and circulated a questionnaire both in Somalia and in the large expatriate communities where Somalis had settled in Europe, the United States, the Middle East, and Africa. The data collection took nine months, but eventually a panel familiar with the various clans, elders, and families screened all the resumes we received, and verified the accuracy of every contact.

The final, published *Directory of Somali Professionals* is a 130-page volume with over 600 entries, and provides details on each candidate's education, language skills, employment experience, and ability to return to Somalia to participate in development projects. It includes professionals from all applicable disciplines: medicine, agriculture, veterinary science, fisheries, security, architecture, economics, journalism, political affairs, and more.

The effort realized initial success in hiring Somalis who knew the language and culture of the country and were willing to work at a fraction of the cost of foreign experts. Sadly, the eventual total collapse of Somalia into a failed state left the *Directory* in limbo for successive decades; nevertheless, the project did provide a model for our later training efforts and proved to us the importance of selecting local personnel, who are far more likely than international aid workers to remain in troubled areas and, ultimately, train new humanitarian leaders.

II.   Landmine Projects

In the post-Cold War world, the enormity of the global landmine crisis generated public demands for action. But what action should be taken? What could be done?

I had seen the landmine crisis firsthand as a physician directing medical and public health programs in the war zones of Nicaragua, Somalia, and the Sudan. I had treated the mutilated, the blinded, and the psychologically traumatized, and witnessed the devastating effects of landmines on affected families, communities, and countries. The CIHC was determined to play a role in finding solutions to this modern scourge, while also providing assistance and comfort to those whose lives had been affected by landmines.

Jaipur Foot Project

To assist landmine victims, and to develop a simple and inexpensive prosthetic program that could be replicated in other poor, war-torn areas, the CIHC began an amputee project, first in Nicaragua and later in Hargeisa, a city in northern Somalia. In the latter site, within four months, and employing only handicapped Somali veterans, we constructed a rehabilitation facility and trained unskilled technicians to fit pre-formed "Jaipur Foot" limbs. Board Member Paul Hamlyn brought these inexpensive, lightweight prosthetics to the CIHC's attention, and provided an initial grant of $100,000 for the project.

It was no small feat to establish an entirely new health facility in a war-torn and unstable area of northern Somalia. The fledgling local government barely functioned, and the nearby towns and villages had been leveled, with more than 80 percent of Hargeisa's buildings uninhabitable. Electric power stations and telecommunications had been destroyed. Health, education and sanitation services were almost non-existent, and roads were extremely insecure and difficult to traverse.

However, the CIHC believed that if we could establish a successful amputee program in such a chaotic setting, the facility would not only provide assistance to the neglected disabled, but also serve as highly visible sign of public health in action. Few examples of a functioning health service are as dramatic as hundreds of formerly handicapped persons suddenly able to walk around town (fig. next page).

Four factors, learned from observing the failures of the past, including many of our own in a previous effort in Nicaragua, helped ensure our success in Somali:

This young Somali girl was the first double amputee I fitted with "Jaipur" feet. Within a day of being fitted with these below the knee, twelve-dollar, polyurethane prostheses, she could walk. A year later, she was chosen to go to a UN conference on landmines in Geneva, Switzerland. As she walked across the stage to be photographed with the UN Secretary-General, she, who had never been on an airplane or in a hotel, had never seen snow or an auditorium full of clapping diplomats, froze in panic. Then she recognized me in the audience and ran from the stage into my protective arms, crying in Somali, "Daddy, Daddy." Experiences like that make all the hard, lonely, and often frustrating field work worthwhile.

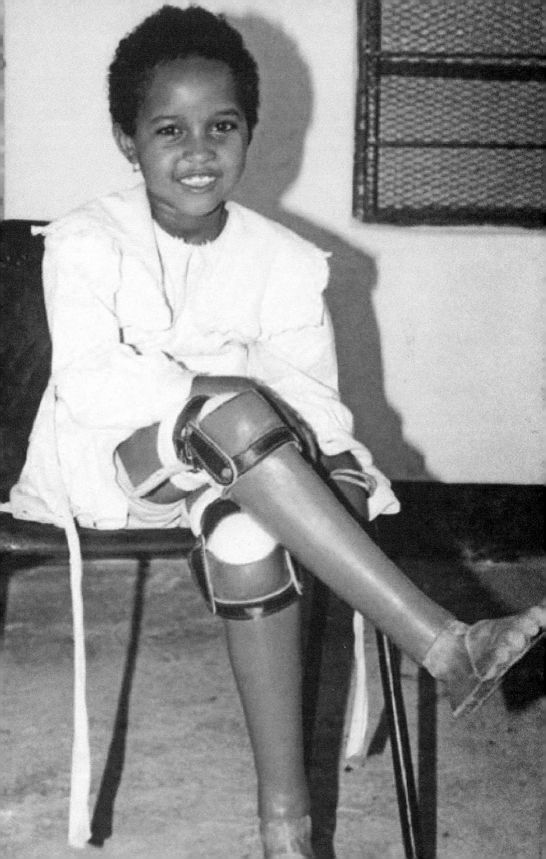

1. We established the rehabilitation center as an operation run entirely by local Somalis. To that end, Somali personnel were involved from the start in the planning, execution, and operation of the project. We lived up to our local motto, "Help the Somali people help themselves."

2. We ensured our center would be effective and relatively inexpensive to operate, and would fall within the resource capability of a local government to sustain once conditions returned to normal. The African Development Bank provided a grant of $350,000, and we made sure not to spend those limited resources on expensive foreign training programs or overqualified staff. Abdulrahim Abby Farah moved to Hargeisa as Resident Administrator for nine months to oversee the project. I made three lengthy trips to Northern Somalia to assess the progress of our program.

3. The services offered by the Center were available to all amputees free of charge and without discrimination of any kind.

4. To ensure the humanitarian and nonpolitical nature of the project and its managerial independence, we avoided formal governmental involvement.

The CIHC program in Somalia demonstrated that, with modest resources and rapid training, a successful outcome could be achieved that benefited both landmine victims and the community as a whole, and could be replicated elsewhere in impoverished post-conflict zones with inadequate medical services. The Amputee Program in Hargeisa was eventually turned over to the Norwegian Red Cross, and is still active 24 years later, assisting countless amputees with prosthetics and physical therapy. The CIHC was able to remit $35,000, a most unusual experience according to a senior Bank official. The CIHC is extremely proud of this legacy.

Clearing the Fields: Solutions to the Global Landmine Crisis (1994)

In search of answers, or at least the right questions, to the landmine crisis, the CIHC and the Council on Foreign Relations (CFR) brought leading authorities together to present their ideas at a symposium in New York City in the spring of 1994.

The conference and resulting book, *Clearing the Fields*, continued the CIHC's effort to promote a multidisciplinary approach to global problems that no longer fell neatly into the old pigeonholes of power politics, conventional diplomacy, medicine, or public health. Our premise was that in most contemporary international crises, specialists in many apparently unrelated fields were as relevant as foreign affairs or traditional medical experts.

Clearing the Fields was an effort of men and women, in and out of government, representing different disciplines and ideologies, all searching for solutions to a universally recognized disaster.

One of the CIHC's later Occasional Papers provided details of a further diplomatic effort to ban cluster bombs, which eventually developed into the Ottawa Mine Ban Treaty, an agreement signed by over 140 nations. Unfortunately, the major powers failed to sign, and now, two decades since the approval and adoption of that treaty, which prohibits the use, production, and export of mines and provided legal obligations to support the clearing of mines, these horrific weapons still crop up in war zones, most recently in Yemen. Despite tremendous progress, international consensus remains out of reach, and the effort to eradicate landmines and assist the victims continues.

Silent Witnesses (1995)

As a physician, I believe that words alone cannot adequately capture the pain and loss of limbs, or the incredible courage and resiliency of amputees. When the UN asked that I prepare a visual presentation on the Jaipur Foot project in Somalia for a major international conference on landmines, I felt that my own amateur photographs would not suffice. Instead, I planned a first-rate photographic exhibit that would complement the words of *Clearing the Fields*.

I recruited photographers who were friends and patients, hoping their artistic eye could further illuminate the terrible destructive nature of land mines. The first photographer I contacted, Thomas Roma, immediately understood the potential of a documentary project that would reveal the basic inhumanity of the situation without exploiting the victims. Working together, we drew up a list from the top ranks of fashion, journalism, documentary, and fine art photographers.

Twenty-five internationally acclaimed photographers contributed their unique impressions of the horrible impact of landmines. All were given the same challenge: they received several prosthetic limbs and five days to produce their photographs. The result was in the grand tradition of Goya and Picasso: diverse artists confronting a man-made scourge. Dr. Robert Coles, the noted author and child psychiatrist, described the result as "a compelling and haunting group of photographs that bring the full horror, the utter depravity of a kind of human murderousness to the reader's attention."

The exhibit opened at UN Headquarters in New York and traveled the world for six years. Eventually, the photographs were sold at auction, with profits going toward a charity to support landmine victims. Perhaps, after all the words are forgotten, only art endures.

As Secretary-General Boutros Boutros-Ghali movingly wrote in his Foreword to the book, "*Silent Witnesses* is testimony to the human price that will continue to escalate as long as land mines persist on our earth and breed silence—not the silence, as the poet said, that follows music, but the silence of no more music."

III.   Early Conferences and Publications

When the CIHC was founded in 1992, the world had just emerged from the Cold War, and all was in violent and tumultuous transition. Old regional and international arrangements that defined a generation had been swept aside, leaving uncertainty and, at times, total chaos. Humanitarian workers desperately sought alternatives to the traditional tools of diplomacy. It was the belief of the CIHC that humanitarian actions could open doors to negotiated settlements and build permanent bridges to peace, even in the midst of violence.

It was in that spirit of possibility that the CIHC convened a symposium in the fall of 1992 at the CFR in New York City. The symposium, entitled "A Framework for Survival: Health, Human Rights and Humanitarian Assistance in Conflicts and Disasters," brought specialists in foreign affairs together with leaders in the fields of international law, medicine, and disaster aid. The premise was that both groups had a great deal to contribute to each other in the common cause of providing better assistance to the victims of wars and natural calamities, and in developing policy initiatives that could lead to the peaceful resolutions of conflicts and the prevention of mass suffering. As I wrote in this book, "We are inextricably linked on this earth to the fates of all the innocent victims of oppression... I am convinced that by cooperating in efforts to heal the wounds of war and eliminate the causes of widespread violence we can find new ways to peace, approaches that are more promising than the alliances and military force that have dominated international relations through so many troubled years."

The CFR in New York is often considered "the second State Department" because of its influence and members. As one of those members—and as the first physician so honored—I developed a close relationship with the organization. Peter Tarnoff, one of our Directors, served as US Under-Secretary of State in several administrations, and after leaving government service, acted as President of the CFR.

Preventive Diplomacy (1996)

Another major philosophic foundation for the CIHC was the conviction that the methodology of public health and the semantics of medicine could be applied, beneficially, to the understanding and practice of diplomacy. A high-level, two-day conference exploring this approach was convened at the UN in 1995 (fig. next page). A resultant book has gone through several editions and has been translated into French with a Foreword by Bernard Kouchner, the co-founder of Médecins Sans Frontières (MSF) and later the Foreign Minister of France. Since the topic was once again the basis for a major UN Conference in 2017, the concluding chapter of this book is on preventive diplomacy (page 157), linking our earliest efforts with our most recent work.

A casual photo of an early CIHC conference. Cyrus Vance (center) was the former US Secretary of State and a Founding Director of the CIHC. In his later years, he was outspoken on the neglected significance of health and humanitarian issues in foreign policy. Peter Hansen (left) was then the UN Under-Secretary-General for Humanitarian Affairs (OCHA). He later served for nine years as Commissioner-General of UNRWA, and became a Director of the CIHC and Diplomat in Residence at Fordham's IIHA.
Dr. Kevin M. Cahill (right) is the author of this book and President of the CIHC.

The Role of the University

Over a lifetime, I have tried to distill experiences on the front lines of humanitarian crises—whether due to natural disasters, or as the inevitable side effects of armed conflicts—into acceptable university programs. In doing so, I have aimed to redefine humanitarian relief work as not merely the actions of "do-gooders," but as a distinct new profession, and to confer legitimacy on humanitarians who seek to build bridges to peace and understanding in times of war. Only academia is empowered to confer diplomas and degrees, and establish standards that are universally recognized.

Starting early in the 1960s, the complex demands posed by the chaos of refugee camps inevitably became part of my duties as a physician working in war-torn areas of Somalia, Sudan, and Central America. By the 1970s, after the Sahel drought, I managed camps that held over one million refugees and internally displaced persons (IDPs) in Somalia.

This responsibility superseded the purely clinical and public health practice I had previously accepted as my professional role. No longer could I focus solely on the life cycles of parasites, the detection of specific diseases, the establishment of medical therapies, or even on the prevention of illnesses. I had become enmeshed in a profound cultural drama between the developed and developing worlds, and in the philosophic and programmatic efforts to promote justice and peace in an unfair world.

Physicians are accustomed to offer diagnoses and treatments based on scientific analyses and clinical measurements supported by various laboratory, radiographic, and technical tests and procedures. Modern Western-trained medical personnel rarely alter their therapeutic recommendations to accommodate cultural factors; however, in international disaster relief operations, particularly in complex humanitarian crises, cultural factors and other outside forces are of paramount concern.

My experiences in the field often ran counter to the established didactic methods so easily accepted as doctrine in a Western medical school. In delivering humanitarian assistance, one must learn to approach those in pain in a nonjudgmental manner. Relief workers must leave behind their pride, their preconceptions, and sublimate their own interests and agendas in an act of solidarity with refugees and displaced persons. They must learn to tread softly, to offer change with great care. Existing customs and practice in any community, especially in the chaos of refugee camps, must not be altered without consultation and deliberation.

When I first began working in complex humanitarian crises, there were almost no accepted standards. In fact, there was not even a common vocabulary. What was desperately needed was the creation of a new profession, one that could embrace the many areas of expertise required to provide an overall response. This is where academia had to enter the picture.

It is primarily in the university where knowledge is analyzed and defined, where good and bad practices are studied, where the lessons of the past are examined in a continuing search for wisdom and understanding. Humanitarian assistance is an ideal area for academic interest. It presents a multidisciplinary challenge and draws upon the fields of public health and medicine, law and politics, logistics and security, technology and anthropology; indeed, all the social, physical, moral, economic, and philosophic arts and sciences.

Society has entrusted universities with establishing rigorous standards to assure good practices. In almost every nation, for example, one must pass an academic exam to practice as a physician or a lawyer; in the United States, one must even qualify, by government testing, to become a plumber or a hairdresser. Yet no such standards or certifications were required of humanitarian workers. One only had to have, or contend to have, compassion and a self-anointed ability to assist those in need.

I sadly discovered, as a medical doctor working in refugee camps, that a not insignificant percentage of humanitarian workers were primarily there to fulfill their own needs, to gratify their own dreams, to satisfy a distorted sense of redemption in a place of chaos. Many had no training, few skills, and even few inner resources to sustain them. These deluded volunteers complicated relief efforts, often causing more harm than good. An inordinate amount of time was spent helping to extricate these "humanitarians" from refugee camps, draining vital energies that should have been devoted to the real victims of disasters.

Such experiences led me to the university to establish consistent requirements for appropriate training for all, whatever their other skills, who presumed to enter turbulent zones of disaster and share in the inordinately rewarding task of dispensing critical assistance.

The university should be, and usually is, the last bastion of free speech, where open discussions and respect for differing ideals prevail. It is society's ultimate refuge from bias and prejudice, and these are among the most significant causative factors in humanitarian crises. The search for answers in such crises cannot be limited to a medical school, or a law school, or any other specialized school. It involves all the many, interlinking fields of study that are the foundation of a true university.

In 1997, the CIHC formally established a university link, first with Hunter College of the City University of New York (CUNY), and later with Fordham University in New York, where we were incorporated as an independent Institute. The CIHC previously had a similar arrangement with the Royal College of Surgeons in Ireland (RCSI), where I served as Chairman of the Department of Tropical Medicine and International Health. As our teaching programs increased, we also developed formal ties with the United Nations University, the University of Geneva, and other institutions of higher learning.

The IDHA Experience

The primary purpose of the CIHC, from its inception, has been to train and prepare humanitarian aid workers. Our early years were necessarily a time of experimentation, as we attempted to define an appropriate educational approach, while still maintaining field operations that provided legitimacy and expanded our contacts within the international relief community. Just as importantly, we had to secure a fiscal foundation before we could hire a project manager, offer scholarship aid, and provide for travel and other expenses. After four years, we were ready for that next step in the process, and we started to search for possible candidates to fill the project manager role. Both Cyrus Vance and David Owen suggested "an interesting man" with the UN High Commissioner for Refugees (UNHCR) in Sarajevo, and we were soon in contact with Larry Hollingworth.

At the time, Larry was a retired British army officer with 30 years of intensive experience in conflict zones. I soon discovered, to my delight, that he not only understood the multiple elements of humanitarian relief in all its complexity, but also he could teach that material to others in a compelling manner, perhaps the result of his training as an amateur Shakespearean actor earlier in his life. His luxurious white beard, adopted after he left the military, only added to the dramatic effect; I later learned that the children of war-torn Bosnia referred to him as "Father Christmas," a not inaccurate description of his appearance and caring personality.

I eventually tracked Larry down in Chechnya, where he was then stationed, and I knew immediately that he shared my vision of humanitarian assistance. I asked if he would be interested in a full-time position with the CIHC, and quickly enlisted him as a unique partner for our projects. Larry is now a trusted friend, and one of the most honorable, compassionate, and competent colleagues with whom I have had the privilege to work over a lifetime of academic and public service positions.

Shortly after he accepted our offer, Larry joined us in a small beach town outside of New York City, and we spent several days discussing the needs of field workers, and structuring comprehensive training, various curricula, and feasible course schedules for students who could not take extended time off from critical assignments.

We aimed to teach men and women with expertise in all disciplines related to complex humanitarian response, and we especially sought those who already had field experience and who showed the potential to lead a new generation of aid workers. Michel Veuthey, then the Chief Counsel of the International Committee of the Red Cross (ICRC), also participated in some of those early, memorable meetings. Within the year, Larry had fully committed himself to the CIHC, and we success-fully launched our inaugural IDHA in Dublin, Ireland.

Larry has been the Director for all 50 IDHA courses and dozens of specialized educational programs, which we offer in locations across Europe, Africa, Asia, and the Americas. In addition to his directorial responsibilities, Larry has assisted UN emergency relief projects in Aceh, Beirut; the Jenin camp in Palestine; East Timor; Baghdad; Kashmir; the Dadaab camp in Kenya; and, most recently, Yangon. The CIHC has fully funded his participation in all of these projects.

In 2011, the US Department of State awarded Larry its highest honor for lifetime service to refugees. The citation read in part, "In times of war and catastrophe, some people lose their moral bearings. But others find themselves a compass that steers a true course through fear and chaos. Larry Hollingworth is one of those people."

To our alumni, Larry is the steadfast, disciplined, wise, and loving face of the CIHC. To me, he has been an indispensable partner and loyal friend for over 20 years, and words alone cannot possibly capture my gratitude and respect for him and his wife, Josie.

Larry Hollingworth

From 1992 to 1995, Lord David Owen served as the EU peace negotiator in the former Yugoslavia. Over the course of those three years, he witnessed a number of humanitarian agencies respond to the crisis, with varied success. Both he and his UN counterpart, Cyrus Vance, concluded that a wide disparity of experience and aptitude existed among the individual aid workers at the crux of the response, and as Board Members of the CIHC, the two men decided to share their observations and concerns with Dr. Cahill, which led to a candid discussion about the current challenges facing the humanitarian aid community. These challenges, all three unanimously agreed, had produced a critical need for a professional qualification course for humanitarian aid workers, one that held international recognition, and that would provoke more profound approaches to crises and conflicts.

My journey with them began with a phone call from Dr. Cahill, and then from Lord Owen. At the time, I was the head of the UNHCR office in Dagestan, where I oversaw the repatriation of refugees displaced from the Chechen conflict. Lord Owen asked me if I could come to London to talk about the possibility of establishing a humanitarian course—and, as one could imagine in my current post, I did not need much of an excuse to visit London.

I could hardly contain my excitement for the idea, and at the end of our meeting, Lord Owen suggested that I speak further with Dr. Cahill in New York. I followed up immediately and shortly thereafter, I traveled to New York, where Dr. Cahill and his wife, Kate, graciously offered to host me at their beach house in Point Lookout. As we sat around the dinner table, I became acutely aware that I was in the company of two extraordinarily accomplished individuals. Dr. Cahill, as both a doctor and a humanitarian, could lay claim to a remarkable array of skills, and his good lady Kate, in addition to being an excellent host, was both a talented artist and poet. Now, almost 20 years later, I realize that this meeting marked the start of a wonderful professional relationship and a valuable friendship. I had no idea that together we would travel so far and for so long, and with such success.

Eventually, the conversation turned to humanitarian aid and the specifics of the qualification course. We quickly realized that what humanitarian aid workers truly needed was a "license to operate," so to speak—a means by which employers, fellow aid workers, and beneficiaries could certify that the holder of the license was a competent field operator. We decided that the course could not last longer than one month, the maximum period that agencies would release their employees from field service. As for the distinguishing qualification, we looked at requirements for various universities and discovered that students had to complete at least 200 in-class hours to qualify for a postgraduate diploma. For a month-long course, this would amount to 50 hours of class time a week, which, while admittedly intensive, would come to the same number of on-duty hours that humanitarian professionals typically complete in the field.

The course would be heavily academic, incorporating theoretical knowledge and historical content, but all the subjects would be directly applicable and relevant. It would be a "hands-on" field course, with a strong technical and practical content. In order to achieve this end, we understood that the teaching staff would have to include highly experienced field operators. Since our approach to humanitarian education was unique, so too would be our course structure. We decided that to maximize student interaction, we would establish a tutorial system in which we would divide the class into small "syndicates" of students, each led by a tutor with a wealth of practical humanitarian experience and the ability to teach.

Now that we had devised the approach, the structure, and the method, all that was left was for us to secure the academic endorsement and official backing of an educational institution. Fortunately, Dr. Cahill at the time was Professor of Tropical Medicine at the RCSI, and upon hearing the details of this new "humanitarian initiative," the College graciously agreed to authenticate a postgraduate diploma after 200 hours of tuition. We were off!

The first IDHA took place in the July of 1997, in Dublin, Ireland. In the run-up to the event, we faced three administrative problems: venue, teaching staff, and students. The first was easily solved as the RCSI offered to host our inaugural course on its campus. As for teaching staff, we began to phone all of our well-qualified colleagues and friends who possessed the prerequisite field experience and offered them a trip to Dublin to join us. Some of the lecturers who took up that initial offer, like Tony Land, continue to work with us and support the CIHC, some 20 years later.

Once we secured a teaching staff, we turned our attention to our third problem: finding students who would be willing to participate in a brand new course. Committing to an untested, four-week program demands an immense leap of faith, and we recruited heavily from the CIHC rosters of individuals and teams that previously worked with us. To this day, I am so thankful for those who trusted us and took that leap of faith. You were the pioneers, and you will always hold a special place in the history of the IDHA.

The RCSI was the ideal place to hold our first course. Founded in 1784, the College sits in the heart of Dublin. Its halls are steeped in history, and the campus boasts a magnificent auditorium, of which we took full advantage. The students stayed in university accommodations. IDHA 1 was a memorable and thought-provoking inaugural course, one that left us feeling as if we had discovered a wealth of untapped potential, and we returned to Dublin twice more over the next decade.

We held the second IDHA in New York, the home of the United Nations, and the residence of many of our dear friends and colleagues. The President of Hunter College, David Caputo, with whom Dr. Cahill is well acquainted, found us accommodation at the Nursing Training College. Women lived in one corridor and men in another, an arrangement that no doubt called to mind childhood classrooms and college dormitories. The residence featured a recreational area in the middle, which one of the students, Cecilia Vazquez, decorated at her own expense to make everyone feel a bit more comfortable in their home away from home.

Professor Debbie Lucchese was our daily link and she made us very welcome. Every day, the students and teachers took a bus to the Hunter campus, an incredibly vibrant location. The campus was a wonderful place to teach and make new friends; the corridors bustled with activity, and students crowded the dining rooms at all hours.

IDHA 2 hosted a number of incredible speakers, most memorably Sérgio Vierra de Mello, then the head of UNOCHA, who delivered the graduation address. The course also introduced us to a pair of women who remain loyal contributors and friends of the IDHA to this day: Argentina Szabados and Lejla Hrasnica. I had worked with Tina in Chechnya, and Lejla in Bosnia. Both women have helped develop

41

and advocate for the continued success of the IDHA, and are active members of our alumni networks. Tina now serves as a member of the CIHC Board and as Chairperson Emeritus of the IDHA Alumni Council, while Lejla is the current Chair of the IDHA Alumni Council.

IDHA 2 was the first course that featured an active civil military element, thanks to a Canadian military team kindly provided by General Lewis MacKenzie. I met General MacKenzie in Bosnia, where he had commanded the Sarajevo Sector, and his team provided the first of our rigorous security days, which have become a vital part of the course.

As we continued to expand upon the success of the IDHA, we cast about for suitable locations for future courses. Lord Owen recommended that the next course be held in the European capital of the UN, Geneva. He and I visited the city to find a venue that would be conducive to our unique student population and intensive course load, but did not have much luck until we arrived at the Château de Bossey, an ecumenical conference center situated just north of the city. The moment he stepped through the doors of the chateau, Lord Owen turned to me and said, "This is it." His instincts turned out to be entirely correct: of the 15 courses we have now hosted in Geneva, 12 have been held at the Bossey.

On that scouting expedition, I also met with one of our course lecturers, Dr. Michel Veuthey. Michel, then a senior lawyer with the ICRC, proved an invaluable addition to our team. He not only introduced our initiative to the University of Geneva, which has now hosted the IDHA on three separate occasions, but also arranged for us to teach the inaugural course of the ICRC Training Centre in Geneva. Michel joined us for many iterations of the IDHA, first as a lecturer and then as an academic director, and he has heavily influenced our syllabus and standards. I have many fond memories from those days, from planning the syllabus around the table at Point Lookout with Dr. Cahill, to running our largest course in the Château de Bossey, where his son Brendan Cahill took his seat as one of our more than 70 students.

We continued to seek out locations and venues that would complement the IDHA learning experience, but we returned every June to New York, which quickly became our home base, and the place where we would soon find the new fulcrum of our initiative. We held three courses at Hunter Collegeof the City University of New York. We eventually moved to Fordham University at the invitation of its then President, Father Joseph A. O'Hare, S.J.

Fordham became our home. The Lincoln Center campus, where we lived, learned, and taught each summer, has hosted our course 15 times over the past two decades. Father Joseph M. McShane, S.J., who assumed the role of Fordham University President in 2003, followed in the footsteps of his predecessor, and has been one of our staunchest supporters, offering constant encouragement for our programs and initiatives, and enthusiasm for our visions for the future.

In 2005, former UN Secretary-General Boutros Boutros-Ghali, then a Board Member of CIHC and a close personal friend of Dr. Cahill, persuaded us to offer a course in Cairo, Egypt. We held the course at the Government School for Diplomats, helmed by Ambassador Dr. Hisham El Zimaity, who became a good friend of the program and its participants. The course in Cairo was full of unexpected surprises: one of our tutors, Gonzalo Sánchez-Terán, who now serves as the CIHC Deputy Humanitarian Programs Director, even ran into the Nobel Laureate Naguib Mahfoouz in the hotel opposite ours!

In 2006, in addition to our now established winter course in Geneva and summer course in New York, the CIHC held our first course in the developing world in Nairobi, Kenya. We stayed in the Karen suburb of Nairobi at the Mary Ward Centre, a small religious compound run by the Institute of the Blessed Virgin Mary, more commonly known as the Loreto Sisters. Aside from its founder, Mary Ward, one of the most well known Loreto Sisters was Mother Teresa, who was part of the congregation before founding her own order.

The Mary Ward Centre was an ideal location: small, safe, and peaceful with an excellent rustic classroom. The compound was enlivened every day by exotic birds singing, tweeting, croaking, and cackling, and the unsettling appearance of the occasional snake. After class, students and teachers could stretch out on the verdant lawns, or relax in the shade of the Jacaranda trees. Sister Anastasia ran the convent with an iron fist. She was universally adored, but unfortunately, she left her position shortly after the course ended.

We held three more courses at the Mary Ward Centre, but none could quite compare to the first. Kenya was the perfect location for our many of our students: not too far to travel, and certainly easier to obtain a student visa there than in the United States or Europe. We recruited a fair number of Kenyan nationals for that course, and pulled in some international students stationed in the region.

That is not to say our regular staff did not take an active role in the course. Lord Owen visited us; Tina Szabados introduced goulash to the cook; and Florian Razesberger, now one of our senior tutors and Course Directors, first joined our team on this course. Valeria Fabbroni, who worked with me in the Jenin camp in Palestine and who now runs the Swiss Mine Action Foundation, and Antonella Scifo, who worked so fearlessly in the field that on one occasion she frightened our African field expert, Gonzalo Sánchez-Terán, acted as our Course Administrators.

We invited some remarkable humanitarian leaders, such as Maina Kiai, an outspoken anti-corruption lawyer, who would speak at our subsequent courses with bodyguards in tow. We also received lectures from Sister Ephigenia Gachiri, a vocal opponent of female genital mutilation in Kenya. Sister Ephigenia offers a local solution to the problem, which is considered a rite of passage for Kenyan women: she sits down with community elders and convinces them to modify the pattern of the ritual for girls. The ritual still occurs in secret, and for the same span of time, but the culmination of the rite is not a dangerous surgical procedure, but a festival in which the girls, dressed in white and with arms full of flowers, emerge from the women's compound to drums and chants.

After the success of our first course in Kenya, Lady Helen Hamlyn, a CIHC Board Member and long-time supporter of our work, recommended that our next location be Goa, India. Lady Hamlyn owns a house in the area, and at the time, had purchased and started renovations on a castle in Goa. In fact, one of my fondest memories from that course is of the reception Lady Hamlyn held for regular staff in her exquisitely decorated home, followed by the sumptuous meal hosted by her neighbor under a vine-covered trellis.

Goa turned out to be a superb choice. The course, hosted at a fine hotel, attracted participants with a diverse set of professional and personal experiences, and a dream team of tutors, many of whom had joined us several times before. The manager of the hotel, Mr. Braganza, did his best to respond to our every request and produced exceptional meals—except, of course, on days when our students pestered him.

The graduation ceremony at the end of the course was truly special. Some of the students and staff—including our Helen Hamlyn Senior Fellow Arancha Garcia del Soto, Tina Szabados and the Course Administrator Kasia Laskowski—had saris made locally for the occasion, and they looked spectacular. Our course student speaker, Father Alexis Premkumar, S.J., sang and held us spellbound, his performance made all the more memorable in my mind because of the terrible ordeal he would soon face.

One year later, in 2011, we decided to run a course in Kuala Lumpur, Malaysia. Al Panico, an IDHA alumnus and the second-in-command at the International Federation of the Red Cross and Red Crescent (IFRC) Asia Pacific Regional Office, believed Malaysia would make an excellent hub for students and lecturers alike. Kasia was very impressed by the on-site support of IFRC and the interest of those in the region.

The following year, our third course of the year, IDHA 38, was also off in a new direction: Pretoria, South Africa. The University of Pretoria hosted us, but we actually held the course in an outpost of the University, in a place called Hammanskraal. It turned out to be a quiet, peaceful location, and we were very much self-contained. The pool was very popular, and we were visited daily by a tribe of monkeys. Despite the presence of some venomous snakes, Kasia and a few of the participants ran around the inner perimeter fence every day for exercise. Our eloquent external graduation speaker was the CEO of the Desmond Tutu Peace Centre, Nomfundo Walaza.

Our next spring course did not take place in Geneva, but in a new location for us: Berlin, Germany. Tina Szabados was Country Representative for the International Organization for Migration (IOM) and with her husband, Dr. Tibor Görög, did all the groundwork to make the course a success. We stayed in a very busy hostel, with a daily turnover of backpackers from all over the world. Tibor was excellent at ensuring that we were priority guests. He visited the course more than once every day. We were delighted to present him with an honorary degree at the graduation. He has a long history with us, due to his family's involvement with the IDHA. He was present when Tina received her diploma 15 years earlier; their son, Zsolt, is an alumnus, and daughter, Ingrid, has taught as a Course Administrator.

For the third course in 2013, we returned to Kuala Lumpur. It was professionally an excellent choice. An earthquake had hit the Philippines only days before our arrival. Our host organization, IFRC, was one of the most important responders, and their operation was directed out of the Kuala Lumpur office. We felt caught up in the response as we heard daily briefs on the progress of the humanitarian response. IFRC Regional Director Jagan Chapagain opened the course, and our graduation speaker was Julia Chong, a successful businesswoman with an NGO of her own.

Over the years, we have also established a solid partnership with the Barcelona International Peace Resource Center, led by Director Jordi Capdevila and his right hand, Eva Lopez Amat; as a result, we have found yet another satellite city. Following a number of successful and popular one-week courses at the Peace Center's training centers, including the spectacular Fort at Mont Juic, we decided to bring the IDHA to the city of Gaudi. It was a popular decision. We stayed in a working convent in a quiet suburb close to the center of Barcelona. The nuns ranged in age, with some in their seventies, and a few even in their nineties.

The rooms were "cells" of various sizes. I was allocated the so-called "Bishop's room," which, despite being the smallest room in the convent, is the only one with a double bed! In the corner of the classroom, which used to be the chapel, there is a concert-tuned grand piano, which was played by the lay administrator of the convent, who is a professional trainer of opera singers. The room has outstanding acoustics and therefore was a wonderful space to lecture. Our Course Administrator, Jill Hamlin, who holds undergraduate and graduate degrees in music, practiced piano every evening, to our great joy.

In 2015, we returned to Geneva in February, then back to New York for June, and off to a new location in November. We decided to run the IDHA for the first time in Amman, Jordan. We chose the Jesuit Centre where we had previously run some one-week courses. Getting the course off the ground was a close thing. Our Course Administrator, Suzanne Arnold, worked miracles as we faced challenges with participant visas and last minute changes to the program due to ongoing humanitarian emergencies in the region. It was a rewarding and truly enriching course, and we had the honor of the presence of the Special Representative of the UN Secretary-General to Syria, Yacoob El Hilla, who flew in from Damascus just to give us an up-to-the-moment briefing.

As the course approaches its fiftieth edition, the locations become no less far-reaching and even more relevant. For IDHA 49, we travelled to Kathmandu, Nepal, a recent victim of a terrible earthquake. The UN Resident Coordinator, Valerie Julliand, opened the course, and a number of our lecturers and participants had recent firsthand experience with earthquake response.

Since IDHA 2, we have tried to hold a security day on every course. The most successful have been in New York, where, thanks to the Fordham military program, and to course military graduates, we have had access to training areas including West Point. The security day is typically long and arduous, but always memorable. The topics covered include map reading, negotiation skills, first aid and hostage taking—it is truly a no-holds-barred day. Of the four IDHA graduates who have been taken hostage, all have told us that our training was essential to their survival. For a while we had military days in Geneva, but the September 11 attack put paid to those. It did not help when we submitted a list of our students' names to the Geneva authorities that included not only an Osama, but also a Jihad!

The three cornerstones of the course are the syllabus, the group work, and our tutor system, and all three are deeply intertwined. The syllabus is hands-on and practical, with the aim that, should a student be posted to a new crisis the day after the course ends, he or she should be equipped to rapidly set up an effective program. Each of our students should know enough about the initial response to a crisis to set a team off in the right direction. They should have a firm grasp of shelter requirements; water, sanitation, and hygiene (WASH) essentials; camp management; emergency health responses; humanitarian law; protection issues; and project management; and they should be able to negotiate, establish an educational program, and ensure the safety of all staff and personnel.

On the first night of our course, the students will introduce themselves at an event supervised by Pamela Lupton Bowers, who served as Head of Training for IFRC, and is now an internationally renowned facilitator and management guru. She observes them with the purpose of assessing their characteristics in order to place them into balanced syndicates. On the second day, each participant is placed into a "syndicate," and for two days, Pamela teaches them team building, leadership, management and presentation skills. By Friday of the first week, the students are ready to present as a group an answer to a humanitarian problem. This exercise is repeated twice more, in addition to plenty of group work in the classroom, in order to simulate the arrival and integration of a new team in the field. Often the students are strangers, and must quickly learn to get on well with each other. More importantly, the team is together for the IDHA field tour. We never change the teams, once assigned; field workers must learn to support each other, no matter their personal differences, and so must our students.

Each syndicate is allocated a tutor for the duration of the course. All IDHA tutors are IDHA graduates; this policy ensures that our tutors know the course backwards and forwards, and heads off any student complaints that the course is too hard or the pace is impossible. If your tutor can complete the course, then you can, too!

The tutor role expands invariably to that of mentor and friend. Pamela and the tutors shape the course, and form the friendships. Each course goes through the "forming, storming, norming" stages. After so many courses, the tutors can predict the signs and the symptoms that will lead to a difficult day. Every group has someone who wants to dominate, but fortunately, every group also has a peacemaker. The role of tutor is coveted. We now have a long list of graduates ready to step into the role and guide new generations of humanitarian workers.

During the period when we only held three courses a year, I had the opportunity to return to the field and keep myself up-to-date. Going back into the field is all a matter of timing. The aftermath of the Iraq War gave me two chances. I entered Baghdad on the first Coalition Provisional Authority convoy in mid-March of 2003. Major General Tim Cross, who was a CIHC Board Member for a time, managed to carve out a place for me on the team responsible for Baghdad Central. I spent my time directing the municipal technical staff assigned to the restoration of water and electricity. My major achievement was the removal of the small mountains of rubbish and rubble piled up throughout the city, which presented a health and safety hazard.

I finished my tour and returned to New York to direct another course. I then joined a UN tour in Iraq, where I was again responsible for Bagh-dad Central and for Hilla. This tour was badly affected by the bombing of the UN building on August 19; I was in Hilla at the time with the majority of my team, but the bomb destroyed the office where we worked and killed my second-in-command, Reza Hosseini, who was a wonderful companion, a hard worker, and a highly respected team member. My son Matthew, who graduated from IDHA 1, was in the building when the bomb went off, but thankfully he was uninjured. Most of the UN team was pulled out, and I stayed on with a smaller team until a second bomb exploded in late September, and we were forced to evacuate.

My next tour was to respond to the earthquake in Pakistan. Here my assistant was Rebecca Richards, who was outstanding, and whom I had no trouble recruiting for the next IDHA. She now is running the World Food Programme (WFP) office in Amman.

In 2005, Margareta Wahlström, the Deputy Under Secretary of IFRC who often lectured for the IDHA in Dublin and Geneva, asked if I would join her crisis response team in Lebanon. Because the national airport had been bombed and was unserviceable, I had to find my own way into the country with a little help from an elite British military team. It was a frustrating and depressing tour, and I witnessed firsthand the great damage inflicted upon Lebanon in what was essentially a war between Israel and Hezbollah. During the tour, I met Sadig El Amin, the computer king of the UN Office for the Coordination of Humanitarian Affairs (UNOCHA). He participated in the next IDHA course and has returned a number of times as a tutor.

The IDHA continues to push the boundaries of humanitarian educa-tion. As a teaching team, we have prided ourselves on our flexibility, as demonstrated by our rapid response to those who request short, one-week IDHA courses. We have done three such courses in Sudan, facilitated by Sadig. Manilar Oo who attended one of our Nairobi courses while working for the ICRC in Myanmar organized a superb course in Yangon. We started off with 20 students, but by the last day, the class had doubled in size.

In recent years, we have broadened our reach by offering courses in other languages and in hard-to-reach areas. Dr. Cahill arranged the Nicaragua course with Father Miguel D'Escoto, who was the President of the UN General Assembly (UNGA). It was our first course to rely on simultaneous translation. Tony Land and I were also invited by OCHA to run a course in Beirut for Syrian national staff, who would need to remotely run the programs if the international staff were forced to pull out. Recently, Manilar invited me back to Myanmar to run a workshop in which I taught negotiation skills to Shan leaders who were unable to engage in meaningful dialogue with the new regime, whose soldiers continue to harass the local population.

Twenty years and countless memories later, I am still in awe of all that the IIHA has accomplished. The acorn planted by our three founders has matured into a mighty oak, nurtured by the wisdom of the Board Members of the CIHC, past and present; by the firm leadership and compassion of Dr. Cahill; and by the skill of our Executive Director, Brendan Cahill.

When I signed on for the first course, it was my intention—and indeed, that of Dr. Cahill and Lord Owen—that I would help to get the course of the ground and then hand over the reins. The journey has been longer than expected. It has been shared step by step with a panoply of great speakers and great students. Together we have created a family, and individually we are all changing the world.

A toast to the CIHC, the next 50 IDHA programs, and to the staff and students who have made our courses and publications possible. Cheers, and thank you all.

The IDHA Impact

Our IDHA—and other short course—candidates come from varied backgrounds, an appropriate mix reflecting the many skills needed to fashion a response in complex humanitarian crises. The average age of our students is 38, and most are men and women who have had some experience working in relief operations after natural disasters or conflicts. Some are younger and just starting careers in international humanitarian affairs, while a number are senior figures in the aid world who wished to continue their education on current developments. We have taught health workers, military personnel, missionaries, judges, and experts from local and international aid agencies who desired to understand more broadly their roles and potential in crisis situations.

Most of our students return to field positions; some venture on to Master's (and others advanced degrees) in Humanitarian Affairs; others pursue careers that may seem distant to our core work. Our alumni utilize the IDHA spirit in soup kitchens, women's rights groups, and even—as the final contribution in this section demonstrates—in the world of literature and master paintings. The IDHA led one of our married couples to discover a Caravaggio in Naples, and to link his artwork to the basic philosophy of the CIHC and the IDHA. All graduates are valued members of the IDHA family, and a majority of our students remain in contact well after the course ends, thanks to our close-knit and supportive alumni association, and the wonder of the Internet.

With over 3,000 graduates, it was obviously difficult to select a tiny fraction to submit essays for this book. Larry holds many cherished memories of our students over the years, and I worked closely with him to find graduates with different cultural and professional backgrounds who would be willing to contribute their stories, and reflect on the significance of the IDHA in their lives.

Argentina Szabados   IDHA 2

It seems strange to think it now, but there was a time in my life when I was not involved with the IDHA. It seems even stranger to think that a time existed when there was no IDHA, no blue ribbon course for humanitarian workers, no gold standard to which all imitators aspire and have yet to match. My life is richer on many levels thanks to my involvement with the IDHA, and I believe the humanitarian profession and, by extension, humanitarian response today, is of a higher caliber due to the existence of the IDHA.

Over the course of this chapter, I would like to firstly reflect on the four distinct roles I have played in the IDHA. I have been a student, a tutor, the Chair of the Alumni Council, and now a member of the CIHC Board of Directors. Each of these distinct roles has given me a new appreciation for this wonderful course, which creates a richer understanding of the industry within which we work and the humanity we share. I would secondly like to reflect upon not only what I have received from my strong involvement with the IDHA, but also what I have contributed.

While I can't claim to have attended every single IDHA, nor to have interacted with each and every IDHA graduate, I have certainly attended the majority of the courses, and have spoken with or emailed more than half of the alumni. This is something I am very proud of, and is of critical importance.

We have to go back over two decades, to a time before the inception of the IDHA, to really trace my involvement. During the Balkan Wars, I worked for the World Council of Churches, and was accustomed to seeing, several times a day, a commanding and exceptionally knowledgeable bearded man on the BBC and CNN, speaking from places like Sarajevo and Srebrenica. This man, I later learned, was none other than Larry Hollingworth, one of the founders of the IDHA, the Course Director of all 50 courses, and the CIHC Humanitarian Programs Director. I never actually met Larry during that time, despite the fact that we were probably only streets away from one another, but this was my first introduction to him.

It wasn't until 1995 that we finally met in person. I was operating aid convoys in and out of Chechnya from neighboring Dagestan. The demand for humanitarian assistance had reached critical levels, which meant we had to carefully negotiate and arrange our response efforts with parties to the conflict. At a celebratory function for the departing head of the ICRC, I was introduced to Larry, then the new head of UNHCR. Larry and I worked together closely over the next few months, and I quickly grew to appreciate his precise judgment, his sharp political skills, his extraordinary intellect, his rich and unique mode of expression, and his keen sense of humor, all of which served us incredibly well when times were especially tough.

The period towards the end of the 1990s might be remembered as something of a halcyon time. The world was not free of conflict and strife, but the Dayton Agreement brought peace to the Balkans, stability reigned across most of the former Eastern Bloc, regional economies improved, and social mobility increased. It was the time in between the Gulf Wars, when al-Qaeda was largely unheard of, and before the emergence of the Islamic State. Diseases had been eradicated, or at least contained, with better medications; climate change adaptation was the mantra; and there was a more tolerant view emerging on race, sexuality, and toward those with HIV/AIDS.

In hindsight, this was the ideal time for the IDHA to come into being. Humanitarianism—or a collective of humanitarian organizations working in concert to bring aid and find solutions—became a major force in the late 1990s, as crises in Afghanistan, Cambodia, Somalia, Kurdistan, Liberia, Rwanda, Congo, Yugoslavia, and on both sides of the Caucasus created the need for large-scale humanitarian interventions.

The IDHA sought to tap into the enormous experience gained by individual aid workers, and provide a qualification course for humanitarians who, up to that point, had been trained to operate "on the fly" and by instinct, rather according to procedures based on best practice.

The first IDHA was the culmination of months of hard work and discussion between Dr. Kevin Cahill, President of the CIHC; Lord David Owen, the former British Foreign Secretary; and my old friend, Larry Hollingworth. Larry asked me to participate IDHA 1, but the pressure of my work meant that I would have to wait until the next year to attend.

In 1998, I traveled to New York City and participated in IDHA 2. Like many experienced aid workers, I believed my role at the IDHA was to assist Larry and provide my fellow students with real-world examples. I didn't believe I would actually learn or gain anything: after ten years at the coalface, surely I already knew everything.

I was wrong. There was so much to learn and so many excellent professionals to learn from. Dr. Kevin Cahill and Larry were—and are—able to bring together the very best presenters, tutors, guests and lecturers for IDHA events, no matter what the venue. For example, the keynote speaker at my graduation was Sérgio Vieira de Mello, the third UN High Commissioner for Human Rights and the Special Representative of the UN Secretary-General to Iraq, who was tragically killed in the Canal Hotel Bombing in Iraq.

When I think back to that month, I remember we studied six days a week and, in those pre-internet days, we spent a lot of late evenings in the libraries, copying out notes or photocopying the transparencies that were the precursors of today's ubiquitous PowerPoint.

I hope I contributed something to IDHA 2, because I got so much out of it. Apart from a diploma, of which I am still proud, I also met my best friend, Lejla Hransica. Lejla was a fellow student on IDHA 2 and, like me, has continued to work with and contribute to the IDHA. She not only succeeded me as Chair of the CIHC Alumni Council, but is also a frequent course lecturer, and is now pursuing the MIHA—a degree borne from the success of the IDHA.

Speaking more metaphysically, the IDHA changed me. There is space on the humanitarian canvas for organizations with many different specialties and philosophies. There are those who lead outspokenly and those who direct quietly; those whose operations are high-profile, and those which are camera-shy. Aid agencies can be large or small; contribute to donor foreign policy, or eschew tied aid; operate globally or locally. They all add up to a whole greater than the sum of its parts, and the IDHA undoubtedly provides its students with a common syllabus and understanding of this disparate world.

As a humanitarian worker, I felt some antipathy towards the talkers and the people who spent all their time in meetings, close to the officials or combatants that orchestrated or engaged in the very hostilities that affected civilians. NGOs seemed to be the only groups on the ground that offered real physical relief and psychosocial support to suffering populations, and indeed, there is some measure of truth in that assumption. NGOs can often go where larger institutions cannot, thanks to their relationships with communities, churches or other bodies. Still, no matter how well-positioned a local organization is, permanent change is difficult to achieve without the help and affiliation of international organizations, which coordinate and provide a broader view of the possibilities and challenges in the region. This may slow down or even halt progress at times, but a slow and measured approach is always preferable to a chaotic, unplanned aid operation.

Empowered with this new perspective of humanitarian work, I entered the world of international organizations and joined IOM as Head of Office in Budapest, Hungary. While I thoroughly enjoyed and appreciated my time with the World Council of Churches, I have no regrets about my decision to join IOM. At first, the pace and size of operations were very different, and the switch was as much ideological as physical, but I can say without a doubt that it was the right move for me.

Around the same time, I accepted an invitation to become a tutor for IDHA 11 at Château de Bossey, just outside of Geneva (fig. page 60). That, too, was an ideological switch, as I transitioned from the role of a student to that of a teacher, assigned to a group of students from all parts of the world with varying levels of experience.

All tutors have their own styles, and the Course Administrators strive to match the tutors to the groups. I must confess that my own style is quite pedagogic; I am strict, firm, and direct. My main aim, like that of all the tutors, is to ensure that the students work hard, collaborate, seek out the answers to hard questions, and pass the final exam at the end of the month. Tutoring is a lot of hard but incredibly rewarding work, and I enjoyed it tremendously.

I first participated as a tutor for IDHA 11, and that course remains special to me. I have kept in contact with the students in my syndicate, and many have returned as lecturers and tutors themselves. Most recently, Sadig Elamin, a student from IDHA 11, joined IDHA 46 as a tutor in Amman, Jordan.

IDHA 11 is also of special importance to me because it was where I first met Brendan Cahill, the Executive Director of the IIHA at Fordham University, which is now the home of the IDHA. Brendan has remained a true, steadfast, and loyal friend over the years, not only to me, but to all those involved in the IDHA.

The course is held in the Château de Bossey every year, and the center now feels like home to me. It was there where I first met the brilliant and talented Pamela Lupton-Bowers, who, although based out of Geneva, has opened almost each and every IDHA, no matter the location, and who has guided the students through crucial team-building, leadership, and presentation exercises and lectures. Pamela is a dear friend of mine and the recipient of an honorary IDHA, which she could not deserve more.

There is now a plethora of other humanitarian courses at some of the greatest universities of the world, and I wonder at times why the IDHA remains so successful and how it continues to bear fruit year after year. Much of its success comes down to the rigorous academic program and the incredibly high-profile lecturers who attend the course, be it in New York, Geneva, Nairobi, Amman, Nepal, Kuala Lumpur, Berlin, Pretoria, Goa, Khartoum, or Barcelona; but there is also a certain magical element of the IDHA, which comes from the students themselves.

In a standard academic atmosphere, the learning is fairly uniform, guided by the texts and the style of the lecturers—but the IDHA is not a standard academic atmosphere. IDHA students come from NGOs and international organizations alike, and their places of origin read like a list of the world's most troubled regions. In any particular intake, you might have Sunni and Shia Muslims from Iran and Iraq, Catholics and Protestants from Northern Ireland, Darfurians, Somalis, Rwandans, Turks, and Kurds, all rubbing shoulders with Brooklyn hipsters, London punks, Buddhist monks, folk from the Brazilian favelas and forests, shamans, spiritualists, vegans, nuns, and atheists.

IDHA students do not simply sit and listen to lectures; they shape the direction of course. That is the genius of the IDHA and of an interdisciplinary curriculum that combines academic theory with the practical experience of seasoned humanitarian professionals.

After a few IDHA courses, I realized that we needed a formal mechanism to listen to the views of the students, rather than doing so on an ad hoc basis. I suppose it is more accurate to call this mechanism "structured and organized," rather than "formal," as there are no formal IDHA routines. I discussed the idea with Dr. Cahill, Lord Owen, and Larry, and came up with the idea of the Alumni Council, which first met in Nairobi. I worked on the Council for five years, and I thoroughly enjoyed every minute of it. Gonzalo Sánchez-Terán, an IDHA alumnus and tutor who is currently the Deputy Humanitarian Programs Director of the CIHC, served as the wonderful Secretary of the Alumni Board during my tenure as Chair. After a fruitful five years, I stepped down from the position, and my dear friend Lejla took my place.

To truly represent the voices of all the alumni would be a full-time job, in and of itself, but we do the best we can. I believe we have set up a dependable mechanism to help us solicit the views of the students, and act upon their thoughts and recommendations. This mechanism ensures that the content—and indeed, the personality—of the IDHA continually evolve to best fit the needs of our students.

I now have the incredible honor of serving on the Board of Directors of the CIHC. It is a privilege and a responsibility I take very seriously, as I not only represent the Alumni Council, but also make decisions in my professional capacity as a Regional Director with IOM. The voluntary and involuntary movement of people in today's world is arguably the chief humanitarian issue; it cuts through all the major areas of crisis and intervention. Anyone who sets out to study the humanitarian system needs a deep grounding in why migration happens, and how it affects and shapes societies, not just in the confusion and chaos of war, but over years, decades, and generations afterward. In light of this, Fordham University and IOM adopted a Memorandum of Understanding (MOU) in 2016. I was honored to help facilitate the MOU, which our Director General, Ambassador William Lacy Swing, and the President of Fordham University, Father Joseph M. McShane, signed.

I confess that I feel a little overwhelmed when I consider that as a Board Member, I sit in illustrious company, past and present. We would not be where we are today without H.E. Mr Boutros Boutros-Ghali, Paul Hamlyn, Cardinal John O'Connor, and Cyrus Vance, all of whom are no longer with us, but whose influence is present in everything we do. The current Board is equally impressive, full of wisdom and strength, with Dr. Cahill, Lord Owen, H.E. Mr. Nassir Abdulaziz Al-Nasser, H.E. Dr. Francis Deng, Richard Goldstone, Lady Helen Hamlyn, Peter Hansen, Geraldine Kunstadter, Dr. Eoin O'Brien, Peter Tarnoff and Father Joseph A. O'Hare S.J.

The one overwhelming feeling I have from my association with the IDHA, which now spans over 20 years, is one of pride. Not so much in any of my achievements—that is for others to judge—but pride in belonging, truly belonging, to this wonderful movement which does so much to harmonize humanitarian action across the globe, and as such, makes the troubled world a safer place.

The IDHA is a bonding mechanism for humanitarian workers: at some stage during business negotiations between UN agencies, NGOs, military, media, and clergy, the question is asked: "Have you ever heard of a course called IDHA?" When the answer is "Of course, I was on the first ever IDHA to be held in Goa," or "Indeed, I lectured in Fordham," then the ice is broken and a new rapport, and new dyamic, comes into play. The IDHA is not only a bonding mechanism for humanitarian aid workers, but also a networking and information-sharing mechanism. Countless students, lecturers, tutors, and staff have obtained jobs and high-level advice, purely due to connections forged with fellow alumni, lecturers, and tutors.

With over 3,000 alumni now working in the humanitarian sector, I truly believe that the IDHA and other courses developed by the IIHA have achieved critical mass. The courses continues to flourish, but they have also paved the way for an undergraduate Major and Minor in International Humanitarian Studies, as well as a hugely successful Master's program in International Humanitarian Affairs, thanks to Brendan's leadership and vision. Dr. Tony Land, a great friend, a recipient of an honorary IDHA, and part of the IDHA teaching faculty since IDHA 1 in Dublin, is now a Senior Fellow at the IIHA and has taken academic leadership of the MIHA, continually expanding it and making it all the more relevant to the ever-changing world we live in. The demand for, and the incredible expansion of, these additional academic programs is a testament to the prolific success of the IDHA. It is remarkable to think that that the IDHA only came into existence 20 years ago.

I firmly believe that the IDHA, and all those involved with it, will continue to adapt with the times and uphold the excellence which it has now replicated 50 times. My warmest congratulations to Dr. Kevin Cahill and Larry Hollingworth for their successful completion of the fiftieth IDHA course, and to everyone associated with IDHA on this impressive and significant milestone.

Tina Szabados has been deeply involved with the IDHA program from its early days. She graduated with our second class, became a regular teacher and tutor in subsequent programs, and was the first Chairperson of the IDHA Alumni Council. She is currently the Director of the CIHC and the IOM Regional Director of South-Eastern Europe, Eastern Europe, and Central Asia (SEECA).

Alexis Premkumar, S.J.   IDHA 32

On February 22, 2015, I was born again. On that day, I was finally released from captivity.

I was kidnapped in Sohodat, Herat, in Afghanistan on June 2, 2014. I was held captive for eight months and 20 days, during which time I thought constantly of the IIHA family—in part because I was not able to attend my fourth MIHA module, as I had originally planned. I had taken care of all the arrangements for my travel to New York, but in the end, I never made it.

I do believe, however, that the IDHA security training subconsciously helped me cope during that terrible ordeal, and manage the situation with a certain amount of prudence. In order to communicate the importance of the course, I should describe the order of events before the kidnapping.

Afghanistan has experienced war since 1979, and millions of people have had to either leave the country as refugees, or their homes as IDPs. In 2001, with some semblance of governance and stability restored, refugees started to trickle back into the country. Unfortunately, many of these returnees could not return to their own villages, because the Afghan government did not have the capacity or resources to oversee the process. Instead, returnees settled in townships where the government and international organizations could arrange for housing, employment and educational opportunities, and access to other facilities.

At the time of the kidnapping, I worked at a school located in Sohadat. The school was dedicated to the education of Afghan children who sought refuge in Iran and Pakistan, and was supported by the Jesuit Refugee Service (JRS), a Catholic NGO that works with refugees, IDPs, and returnees in nearly 50 countries around the world. On that fateful day, at around half past midnight, I was waiting outside for my staff. The students had gone home after school, and the other teachers and I were ready to leave for Herat, some 20 miles away. Suddenly, a vehicle with four gunmen rushed towards me at great speed. As soon as I saw the gunmen in the vehicle, I ran inside the school, latched the door, and tried to think of escape. A few seconds later, I heard the sounds of shots fired at the school building, and I suddenly remembered my IDHA session on security.

Larry Hollingworth clearly explained to us that life is more precious than anything else and that prudence is extremely important in such situations. I had no doubt that the gunmen had come to kidnap me, a foreigner, and not my Afghan staff. To protect my workers, I came forward and surrendered myself.

They pushed me into the vehicle, and removed my mobile phone, bag, passport, cash, and spectacles—everything, except my clothes. They tied my hands, forced me to lie down, and warned me that they would kill me if I raised my head. I did not react; I was totally helpless. Instead, I concentrated on Larry's advice that humanitarian actors should avoid collateral damage as much as possible.

IDHA 32 was a turning point in my life. From 2005 to 2011, I served as the Country Director of JRS in Tamil Nadu, India, where I worked with Sri Lankan refugees. Country Directors typically serve for six years, and so in 2010—my final year in Sri Lanka—I met with the International Director of the JRS, Father Peter Balleis, S.J., to discuss my future career path.

I am an ordained Jesuit priest. Since 2000, I have worked to provide assistance for indigenous peoples, Dalits, and Sri Lankan repatriates and refugees. The position demanded active involvement in the field, and after a decade of this kind of work, I felt the need to take some time away from ministry and pursue doctoral research. When I spoke to Father Balleis, he suggested that I complete the IDHA and the MIHA as an alternative to research. I agreed, and in the winter of 2010, I attended IDHA 32 in Goa, India. The following year, I arrived in Afghanistan to continue my mission in Herat. Had I not attended the IDHA, I probably would not have taken up a position in Afghanistan, and my life would have taken a dramatically different course.

IDHA enhanced my knowledge of the humanitarian world. The intensive, one-month program provided a unique atmosphere. Humanitarian scholars delivered lectures, and the participants came from all over the world, and from various NGOs and UN agencies. Of the 19 students who participated in IDHA 32, six were from India, two from East Asia, four from Africa, and seven from the United States and Europe.

IDHA taught me that good planning is essential to achieving great things in a short time. Within a month, we were introduced to practi-

cally all the disciplines in the humanitarian field. We learned about
the humanitarian legal framework; the Sphere Project; Millennium
Development Goals; humanitarian reform; camp management; WASH;
education; project cycle management; psycho-social issues; diseases;
negotiation; community participation; nutrition; civil-military cooperation; media; security; and related subjects.

Educational method is as crucial as content. IDHA 32 had five residential and one visiting staff, and although six years have passed since I
attended the course, the presentations from Larry, Arancha, Florian,
Gonzalo, and Tina are still fresh in my mind. All of them have outstanding records in the field or in academia, and all are gifted with effective
communication skills. Kasia, our administrator, organized the program
from start to finish, and always had a smile on her face. I also learned from
the interactions between students, all of whom represented different
humanitarian fields. IDHA respected the opinions of all the participants, and encouraged these interactions through case study presentations, simulations and debates.

IDHA is special to me. I used to feel too shy to share my thoughts in
front of a group, even though I had many thoughts in mind. I clearly
remember a class in which we had to debate the international sanctions on Iraq. Until then, I was not well known to my peers, but I
prepared well and presented with conviction. I constructed my arguments from the perspective of the people who suffer due to war—all
the sessions at IDHA aimed to bring dignity, security, peace and justice
in the world—and our team won the debate. Perhaps my presentation
is the reason why the IDHA staff selected me as the student speaker
at the graduation ceremony. I was not highly proficient in English, but
I have worked closely with refugees and, to a certain extent, I understand their pain.

During the course, I spent time reading, studying, and examining my
preconceived notions about humanitarian issues. Both my experience
in the field and the theoretical knowledge I gained from the IDHA
lectures helped me discover my own skills as a debater and a speaker.
The IDHA presentations also broadened my understanding of camp
management and directed me to approach the plight of refugees from
a human rights perspective.

In Sri Lanka today, there are more than 60,000 refugees, accommodated in 106 temporary camps. The Sri Lankan Tamils, displaced by war almost 30 years ago, live as refugees in India, in huts and dilapidated houses which offer little privacy and space. This population is under the constant surveillance of special police known as Q Branch, and the freedom of speech and freedom of movement within the camp is severely restricted. Even so, the Indian public generally believes that refugees are treated more humanely than the Dalits and indigenous peoples of India.

The war in Sri Lanka ended in 2009, and still no solution has been proposed for the Tamil refugee situation. IDHA motivated me to reflect on durable solutions, and the knowledge I gained in class and through assignments inspired me to conduct sessions among the refugee youth on the same topic. JRS does not interfere in the decision-making process of the refugee community, but at the same time, we feel a responsibility to help vulnerable populations make informed decisions.

I plan to complete the MIHA in the spring of 2017. I previously completed the International Diploma in Operational Humanitarian Action (IDOHA) in 2012 and the International Diploma in the Management of Humanitarian Action (IDMA) in 2013. The content of these courses had a profound impact on my ability to provide services in Afghanistan, which is one of the most dangerous countries for international humanitarian aid workers.

My staff and I do our best to stay safe, and at the same time, we try to fulfill the mission of the JRS "to accompany, serve and advocate the cause of the refugees." We do not own vehicles, but use taxies to avoid being easy targets. We also do not seek police or any other protection, but believe in the protection of God and the Afghan people. We have a guidance manual on how to safeguard ourselves, and we live under constant constraints regarding freedom of movement and speech.

To be able to leave Afghanistan and attend MIHA courses was itself a great relief. The courses were designed in such a way that we were able to share our experiences with other participants and learn from each other. MIHA courses provided a platform to examine my experiences and engage in the action-reflection paradigm. The Course Directors encouraged us to write assignments based on experiences from the field. For example, I wrote an assignment on collaborative leadership based on my experience on the JRS Training Leaders for Tomorrow program. Linking field-based reflections with appropriate theories helped me assess the benefits and drawbacks of the project. In the end, MIHA courses helped me evaluate my own work better in Afghanistan.

My research thesis for the MIHA focuses on peace building among the Sri Lankan refugees in Tamil Nadu, and the educational engagements of the JRS in that community. It is an opportune time for peace building in Sri Lanka: the war ended in 2009, and a relatively stable government has been in power since 2015.

Many expressed joy at my release. I received phone calls, emails, and visits from IIHA staff and alumni, and I was touched by the short video posted by the members of IDHA 44, welcoming me home. "Letters to Prem," a letter-writing campaign initiated by Brendan Cahill and Kasia after my release, is another masterpiece I cherish very much.

When I think of my journey with the IIHA, I think of the many challenges I have faced over the past six years, as well as the many moments of grace. I am proud to say that the IIHA family walked with me during these moments, and rejoiced with me at my release. The IIHA has broadened my worldview and given me a global perspective of humanitarian issues, for which I am truly grateful.

Florian Razesberger   IDHA 20

When I first learned about the IDHA, I was advised that it was probably not for me. A friend was taking the course at the time, and she thought that with my profile and background, I should look for a different course. "After all, you are a lawyer," she said.

I am, in fact, a lawyer by education, and my work always has had some connection to legal issues; however, I have never been content to sit in a corporate office, trading my lifetime away for money I did not need. To be reduced to the stereotype of a lawyer—tough but boring, a technical stickler, colorless in suit and humor, unscrupulous, and most importantly, greedy—annoys me to no end.

I decided to apply to the IDHA for the same reason I decided to study law a decade earlier: curiosity. Back then I had absolutely no idea what law was about, but when I applied to the IDHA, I thought I had at least some idea about humanitarian assistance. After all, the work I had done as a lawyer always related to situations of conflict, but mostly from a legal side. Yet when I looked at the IDHA curriculum, subjects like humanitarian reform, logistics, or camp management did not tell me anything. Only on the "law day" was there some beacon of clarity within the whole program. The rest was unknown.

What I knew was the routine of everyday work. At the time, I was working on rule of law issues in Macedonia, preparing trainings on war crimes for judges and human rights workshops for young lawyers. It was time for something different. Winter was coming and November in the Balkans is a rather bleak affair. The prospect of learning about a completely foreign subject for a whole month in a place like Nairobi, with people I had never met, and who came from different fields and from countries I had never visited, was a "no-brainer." My boss initially suspected that all of this was a cover for a safari trip and a vacation on the Mombasa beaches, but eventually he agreed to let me go for the month.

It turned out to be a different kind of safari. Someone once referred to the IDHA as a humanitarian boot camp, and there is certainly some truth to this. My colleagues in Macedonia suspected that I would be having idle fun among giraffes and white sand, but that was not the case.

To be basically locked up in a compound, which took the innocent shape of a convent run by caring nuns; to be put to work for four weeks in a row; to come up time and again with reasonable, presentable products; to take exams every Monday; to write a research paper over the weekends; and to sit in class 50 hours each week while staying up until the wee hours with colleagues in order to prepare presentations each Friday—that can be a hell of a ride. Especially when raw emotions take over, exhaustion caused by information-overload creeps in, and frustrations mount as, for some strange reason, your team members do not always agree with your opinions.

The formal education I received in the first two decades of my life differed vastly from the education I received from the IDHA. I had learned to be better than others, to measure myself against my colleagues and aspire to beat them; now, as an IDHA student, I had to learn to be a team player. Our teachers told us we would be together for every day of every week, and worst of all, that we would be graded as a group for our output, and not as individuals. Four long weeks lay ahead of me.

It was made clear that everyone would need to take the lead and present in front of the class—no escape there. While I have had to speak in front of people for my work, it was not an activity I particularly enjoyed. It annoyed me, that at the end of the day, I was afraid of public speaking; the larger the crowd, the more nervous I became. I wanted to overcome this fear, so I swore that for the next four weeks, I would always volunteer to present, whatever happened, and no matter how much I disliked it.

The team made sure that there was enough space to practice. For my IDHA the team members included the Course Director, Larry Hollingworth, as well as the four tutors: Tony Land, a highly experienced UNHCR veteran, always with a joke on his lips; Valeria Fabbroni, very Italian and with a uniquely strict kindness; Anissa Toscano, with her hearty smile and sharp precision in each word; and Gonzalo Sánchez-Terán, always with an abundance of passion. The first time I met Larry, he bounced out of nowhere, shook my hand firmly, welcomed me with a big smile, and before I knew what had happened, he dashed to discuss the start of the course with the tutors.

When I arrived, some fellow students were already sitting out on the patio, assessing each other, and deciding with whom they would spend the next month. We chatted about who had worked where, which missions we had already done. Some were eager to compare, others to talk, and a few to listen. Overall, it was a crowd of experienced professionals, of all ages and nationalities, and there was an aura of great interest and expectation.

As students, we all started at the same level, with no significant difference in status. We were a motley crew, with completely different life stories, and different economic, cultural, social, and professional backgrounds. There were a number of humanitarian workers from both local and international agencies; some freelancers; a few lawyers, medical workers, and project officers; a soldier from the UK; a former high-ranking army officer from Benin; and a freethinker from the corporate world. Contrary to the realities of the working world, we were all equals and we were all required to work as a team.

My first takeaway from the course was the value of the syndicate work. Larry opened the course, and offered a passionate outlook of the next four weeks, telling us how much fun our classes would be. I became slightly suspicious, especially when I learned about the notion of the syndicate. As a native German speaker and as a movie nerd, the first time I heard the term "syndicate," I associated the term with crime stories and conspiracy. Before I could ponder any further, I found myself in a syndicate with a nurse and a midwife from Kenya, a Sudanese aid worker, a Canadian IFRC delegate, and an Englishman whose exact subject matter of expertise escaped me.

We were immediately put to work, and I remember vividly how our first assignment as a group immediately turned into a disaster. We had to produce a presentation in 20 minutes, but instead, everyone gazed around at each other, helplessly looking for a leader. No one took the lead, and somebody eventually started doing something while the rest of us watched or tried to appear busy, so as not to be exposed as utterly useless. Our tutor, Gonzalo, observed us intensely, his fingers nervously scratching his chin and his facial expressions suggesting absolute concern. This was not group work; this was the six of us lost in space, passing each other in the dark.

Yet somehow we survived this first test without too much embarrassment, and started gradually adjusting to the course and to each other.

It did not take long before the syndicate taught me that I was arrogant and limited. On the evening of the second day, every syndicate was asked to give a 15-minute presentation on Friday about an assigned topic. We had three evenings to work with our groups, but my first thought was "I can produce better work by myself in an hour than with my syndicate in a week." I was perhaps right about the fact that I could have worked faster on my own, and that the whole process would have been less complicated and possibly less painful than sitting down for several hours every night, debating and trying to see all angles and ends; but in terms of the quality of what I could produce, I was wrong—hopelessly wrong. I completely underestimated my fellow students, based on the condescending notion that my academic background outweighed whatever practical and academic experience they brought to the table. Most importantly, I did not foresee the value and power of teamwork, blinded by an education system that taught me next to nothing about it.

I initially thought that group work could never be the most efficient way to prepare a presentation. Why ask six when one can do it? Coincidently, another syndicate was thinking along the same lines, so I was not alone. One person in that group suggested that she do it all by herself and spare the others the preparation work, and they could then present her results together. Her suggestion resulted in a major argument, as her group members—who naturally all held different views—did not want to adopt the work of the one who volunteered (she, in turn, felt let down and underappreciated for all the work she did).

By Friday, I knew that I knew very little, that I had much to discover, and I had a lot to learn from my fellow students. The days went by and my syndicate moved, like all the other syndicates, through the famous phases of forming, storming, norming, and performing. What stayed with me from that experience were the long nights, the heated discussions, the misunderstandings and occasional fights, and the forming of an unlikely team that against all odds, managed to deliver.

My second takeaway from the course were the talks: the Kenyan nun describing her lifelong battle against female genital mutilation; a British Major General reflecting on his work in Iraq after the US invasion; a Kenyan human rights activist talking on corruption. One student told her heartbreaking story on how she survived the nightmares brought upon her refugee camp by the Lord's Resistance Army. A former army officer challenged the students on his work for a private security company. I remember talks with random people in the heart of the Kibera slum to which we paid a visit; the heartbreaking graduation speech delivered by one of our own; and, of course, Larry's presentations, which turned ostensibly dull subjects into engaging entertainment. I will never forget his impromptu lecture on law after the original speaker canceled, and his ability to capture the attention of the entire class while walking us through case studies of humanitarian disasters.

Memorable speeches demand a magic mixture of passion, knowledge, experience, humor and entertainment; the speaker must be objective, without catering to the ego of the listener. That combination is very rare to witness, and I hoped to gain such qualities by listening to Larry's talks and practicing my own.

The talks helped bind all the disparate elements of humanitarian aid together. It took a while until I figured what the cluster approach meant; how human rights and humanitarian efforts need to be aligned but also separate; how ethical dilemmas are dealt with differently by different actors; how assessments and standards need to evolve; how one field or organization is connected to the other; and how political choices and economic models set the stages. The talks did not provide any definite answers, but rather initiated a way of thinking that forces us to understand the ever-evolving complexity of the field.

The IDHA addressed the big questions: how conflicts came about and how one could effectively deal with them; how to enable humanitarian action to take place; how to question approaches that do not take into account the larger picture. The story of humanitarian relief is enormously difficult and complex, and the solutions are usually not easy or simple.

Larry told us that there was little time to reflect during the course; that the bombardment of facts, figures, background information and anecdotes, and the lack of free time would not allow for deep contemplation. Reflection, for me, came in the months afterwards, and my curiosity continues to open new doors and to explore different perspectives.

By the end of the course, I only wanted to finish. While I remember many small details, stories, and moments from those four weeks, I have no recollection of the last 24 hours of the course. We received our last assignment and had to produce our final presentation overnight. I cannot remember what it was about, how the last hours of syndicate work went by, if it was easy or difficult, or if the final presentation itself succeeded. My brain must have been completely overloaded by then, unable to put any further data in the storage place for long-term memory; but apparently we did it, because I received my diploma along with the rest of my syndicate. Memory set in again when we were dancing in the garden of the convent at the closing party.

I was happy when the IDHA ended, as I was physically and emotionally exhausted, but I was also happy that I had done it in the first place. After all the exams, presentations, and essays, I felt like I had achieved something I could be proud of. It was an intense experience, one I shared with many others, and one that enriched my life. Now my classmates and I can all tell a joint story, which is to me the most special thing about the course.

What I did not know then was that it was just my first IDHA. The following year I was given the opportunity to be a tutor and I returned to Nairobi. To learn from students and faculty alike, to present, to advise and listen, and to see each IDHA class develop its own dynamics, dramas, jokes, and stories is a wonderful thing. The joint story reappears at airports, in the field, and in random chance encounters with other graduates.

I might have been aware of the most important lessons of the IDHA, even before I took the course, but I had not internalized them yet. The IDHA sharpened my ability to work in a team and adapt to a new situation. My journey continued, first to Bosnia and thereafter to Afghanistan. An extended detour over Kosovo brought me eventually to eastern Ukraine, where I worked on human rights and humanitarian issues.

The IDHA was a turning point for me. As I moved to new places and tasks, I felt comfortable taking the lead in certain situations. I became an active leader, despite my insecurities, and over time I became a trainer, a public speaker, and also a manager. The IDHA syndicate work showed me how to communicate better, not only in the context of humanitarian aid, but also as a partner, a family member, and a friend.

Emotions often get the better of us, not only in situations of war and crisis, but also in our everyday lives. The IDHA taught me how important it is to respond constructively and respectfully, and even when you are pushed beyond your personal boundaries, to make rational decisions.

The course was an ideal way to test my limits, to measure myself in situations that push me out of the comfort zone and provide me with the opportunity to grow. It is only when our guard goes down, when we are tired, annoyed, bored, and irritated, that we are able to learn about sides of ourselves we never knew existed.

In the end, the IDHA is about the passionate moments, big and small: the moments in the syndicates, during fights or during jokes; the moments in the classroom, during the talks and during the breaks; the moments in the hours after class and during the sleepless nights. Those I take with me.

I remember one evening in late November of 2007, while I was a tutor in Nairobi. We were sitting down with the head of the Mary Ward Center, Sister Colette, a strong and kind leader whose wisdom was only matched by her unorthodox sense of humor. We had arrived at the closing days of the IDHA. The syndicates were preparing their final presentations, and we had dinner outside of the convent in a cozy restaurant called The Rusty Nail. The question came up if Sister Colette ever had thought to take a different life path, to marry and have a family of her own. I remember her laughter as she said that she questioned her choices all the time. "Yet, when it comes to choices, like marriage," she said, "that is easy. Everyone can get married. That is not the big thing. The point is to make it work, to go through the difficult times and to come out of them again, hopefully unharmed and stronger than before."

I feel it is the same for the work we do.

The IDHA was our first exposure to the world of humanitarian assistance. We were both interested in the field, but realized we needed to have a reasonable amount of clinical experience before we would be of much assistance in that sphere.

We applied to a number of small and large NGOs, but all of them said they could not deploy us to work together, or even to work in the same country. We ended up in China, performing medical retrievals for a global medical assistance company.

We were deployed twice to Indonesia as members of Australian Medical Assistance Teams (AUSMAT), first after the 2005 tsunami and then after the 2006 earthquake. These two early disaster response deployments piqued our interest to learn more about the emergency response sphere, which eventually led us to the IDHA.

Although we would like to say we specifically sought out a course like the IDHA for altruistic reasons, the truth is that we stumbled across the course by chance, mostly because we were looking for a partially-funded educational jaunt to somewhere in Europe. As a condition of Mark's hospital employment, he was entitled to a five-week study sabbatical. While we knew our medical work, we had struggled at times to make sense of "the big picture," and the IDHA seemed to fit what we were looking for. The IDHA was the perfect program for us, primarily because we are both hands on clinicians and the course focuses on practical training of practitioners in the field.

Unlike medicine, which looks for "cures," the world of humanitarian action strives to decrease suffering and better prepare people to cope by improving overall response. Improved humanitarian response occurs when responders—whether local, national or international—are better prepared. It follows then that an extremely important aspect of any response is to ensure those who go to the field are appropriately trained. The IDHA's founding members overall desire was to appropriately train and prepare practitioners intending to work in the field and it is therefore aimed squarely at this task. It teaches practical approaches to solving commonly encountered complex issues.

Given that we are both hands on clinicians and we were actively seeking a course specifically tailored to actual field work, particularly one that would teach us about the whole humanitarian response, not simply a health response that we were already familiar with, the IDHA seemed a perfect solution. Admittedly, another important attraction was that the IDHA was to be taught during winter in Geneva, Switzerland. We figured it was a win-win situation; we would learn more about disaster and humanitarian response while also having plenty of time to ski and have fun. How wrong could we have been? Anyone who has done the IDHA will know very well there's barely time to sleep during that month, let alone ski.

In 2009, we traveled to Geneva and Château de Bossey for IDHA 27. Initially we thought no one would realize we were married; we imagined we would not be allowed to do the course at the same time. Of course the IDHA staff knew—it wasn't hard, given that we have both used the same email address—and when we arrived, we met Maria, who introduced herself and then said, "Hi, you must be the couple from Australia." Then, in his best Australian French, Mark introduced Angie as his husband (he always seems to get the gender of the nouns confused), which resulted in much laughter in Bossey.

The four weeks were exhausting, challenging, fascinating, and rewarding in the most beautiful setting of Bossey. We learnt about how the course came about, mostly with the dedication and hard work of Dr. Kevin Cahill, who continues to work tirelessly to ensure that there are scholarships available for students from developing countries. Larry Hollingworth was our passionate, hard working Course Director, and an exceptionally gifted lecturer. Brendan Cahill and his team work extremely hard linking the IDHA community and developing the short courses, the Master's program, and more broadly promoting the CIHC.

As students, we loved that IDHA was very much developed to assist with practical, on-the-ground training. It gave us an awareness of all aspects of humanitarian response, not just the subjects we were most familiar with. We learned about team building, international law, human rights law, camp management, project cycle management, and so much more. The course involved more work than either of us anticipated, but we loved every minute of it. We laughed and we cried (mostly at two in the morning when trying to finish the Friday morning presentation), and we learned from an amazing group of lecturers and tutors, who all had a wealth of experience in the humanitarian sphere. Of course, Larry, Tony, and Pamela were there to whip us into shape, and there were a number of fantastic guest lecturers, including Lord David Owen, Richard Gordon, Major General Tim Cross, Florian, and many others whom we can't name. Our eyes were opened to the Palestinian issues so eloquently taught by Peter Hansen, the brutality of mines, and so much more.

Bossey was a fantastic place for group bonding. We were in the middle of nowhere and therefore had to make our own parties. This occurred mainly on Friday nights. The euros were collected Friday morning and the fabulous Maria would buy, and hide, the party-making necessities (i.e. the alcohol). That beautiful lady was our savior. Other fun activities included visiting Richard Burton to say hello and have a drink—he is buried "down the road" from Bossey. We also loved walking across an international border on Sunday to visit a French market, an activity that is impossible to do in Australia. On graduation day we were taken by Xavier, one of our tutors, for a wake-up swim in Lake Geneva; given it was February, no one stayed in long.

Most importantly, the IDHA gave us a structured approach and deeper understanding of the whole of the humanitarian world. The course introduced us to an amazing group of people, many of whom still remain our close friends. Our classmates continue to do incredible work in the field and no doubt use many of the skills we learnt in Château de Bossey.

Prior to leaving, Larry very kindly asked us to consider becoming IDHA tutors. Being invited to teach was not only a great surprise, but also a great honor. We were humbled to be involved because the course boasts so many great lecturers and tutors. We enjoyed the course and believed in its ethos, and we were delighted to be able to participate in mentoring and training future students. In 2010, we flew to New York to teach for the first time, and since then we have returned to the US each June.

Being a tutor is different from being a student. There are different expectations and responsibilities. Now you're not just responsible for your own journey but you feel responsible for that of the students. We remember well our first IDHA—it was full of nervous anticipation.

We, as new tutors, were as nervous on the first day as the students. The students bring with them a large amount of experience and we learn as much from the students as they do from us. Being a tutor has its unique challenges. For example, how do you start to separate one group into syndicates when you've only just met people a few days before? There are different backgrounds, professions, cultures, and genders to consider when trying to balance out the syndicate groups. After the students are divided into syndicates, each syndicate is assigned a tutor, who is responsible for mentoring the group. As a tutor, you rely on communication, leadership and management skills to help guide your students through a successful and fulfilling course.

It is not always an easy task, and not all the students are happy. Many have to work, or leave family and loved ones behind for a month, or travel from conflict zones, or perhaps will have no home to return to; all come from different cultures and backgrounds. How do you cope with this? Mostly you rely on your own strengths and weaknesses and experience as a student. Luckily, being a tutor is a shared responsibility, and there is always help at hand should the challenge seem overwhelming.

For us, the most rewarding aspect of the IDHA is that it truly does become a big family. Each IDHA is special and different, and as tiring as the students' experience, albeit in a different way. Having said that, we happily use our holiday leave to support the course. We believe anyone working in the humanitarian space should be trained. The IDHA is ideal for any practitioner who plans to work in the field. It is professional in its delivery and taught by people who have worked, and very often continue to work, in the world of humanitarian assistance. We continue to learn, very often from the students, every time we participate in the IDHA, and we're always happy to share this knowledge with others.

After completing the IDHA in 2010, and within months of returning to Australia, we were deployed with an AUSMAT team to southern Pakistan to assist with the humanitarian response after the floods. The floods resulted in 20 million people being displaced—nearly the entire population of Australia—and it's fair to say the humanitarian response to that disaster was slow for reasons that have been roundly discussed in the literature.

With the knowledge we gained from IDHA, we helped plan the AUSMAT response. This included using locally acquired World Health Organization (WHO) interagency emergency medical kits, standardized WHO diagnostic criteria, working with local clusters, and following Sphere guidelines to name a few. There were a number of challenges, not least because we were a civilian-military team and patient access was controlled by the Pakistan military. However, Pakistan is a country where the military control is a fact of life, and we had to accept this and work within these constraints. In seven weeks, the Australian team saw over 11,000 patients. We helped identify disease outbreaks such as falciparum malaria, worked with the local health facility to manage patients, and reported daily data to the Pakistan Ministry of Health. We liaised with many of the local and international NGOs to facilitate patient referral for more chronic and long-term conditions.

We were delighted to make contact with an IDHA classmate, who was working with World Vision to address malnutrition in a nearby area. She was instrumental in providing a referral pathway for malnourished children and adults. In many ways, the power of IDHA is in the contacts one makes during and after the course. Over the years we have used many IDHA contacts to assist us when planning a health response. We were also fortunate to have an IDHA contact in Islamabad who was also extremely helpful in providing pre-departure planning information.

In 2011, we worked on the initial course to train AUSMAT team leaders in Darwin. For three years, Larry Hollingworth traveled with us back to Australia directly after IDHA in New York. Larry was instrumental in helping shape AUSMAT's involvement in humanitarian response.

As clinicians with special interests in ethical humanitarian response and as members of AUSMAT, attending the IDHA course has had a lasting impact on us both. Not only did IDHA give us a deeper under-standing of the whole humanitarian response but, more importantly, it taught us to question how that response is shaped and work to improve particularly how healthcare is delivered to disaster affected communities.

Who knows what the future holds? For us, we hope to continue our association with the IDHA courses and the IIHA for many years to come. In June 2017, New York will host IDHA 50. It is indeed a great milestone.

Ferdinand von Habsburg-Lothringen   IDHA 9 and MIHA

Many of us need a core set of values in order to anchor our lives and ourselves. I, for one, feel this profound need as I continue to provide humanitarian assistance in the Horn of Africa, after two decades of professional experience in Sudan and South Sudan. I started my career as an aid worker in the 1990s, and I have now crossed through the political landscape of two civil wars. By necessity, I have assumed a leadership role as an actor within the framework of humanitarian and development aid in the region.

My experience has allowed me to witness how human beings, when faced with enormous, apparently insurmountable challenges, continue to seek a way forward; we refer to this strength of the human spirit as "resilience." I have also observed what happens when the interests of the international aid community do not fall into line with the complex demands of the landscape in which I work, with its many peoples and cultures. Above all, I believe that my time in the Horn of Africa has taught me to reflect upon and fairly evaluate the needs of stakeholders, partners, and recipients.

Humanitarians enter into aid work and its different articulations for a variety of reasons, most of which are admirable. However, reminding ourselves of these reasons and retaining our enthusiasm for our work can become difficult as we battle with bureaucracies and insecurity; navigating the emotional and physical minefields of this enormously challenging profession can leave us extremely vulnerable, as well as potentially isolated, in our careers and lives.

Many aid workers come out as "damaged goods," and we struggle to rebuild our sense of self and remain afloat. Three keywords have become central to my work and my life: community, reflection, and change. These words form the very basis of our humanity, and are a call to the future and to action.

"I will call you for one minute." No seven words have held more meaning for me than these; I first heard them on the evening of July 8, 2016, through the crackle of a poor telephone connection.

Years earlier, I had met Dr. Kevin Cahill in his office on the edge of Central Park. I had come for a thorough medical examination, and as he looked me over, he asked me about my work in South Sudan.

Over the course of our conversation, he revealed himself as a consummate thinker, storyteller, and professional, steeped in humility, warmth and humor.

Now, as I crawled on hands and knees across the floor of an office building, ducking under the windows to avoid a storm of bullets outside—a barrage that, I later learned, killed over 250 people—Kevin's seven words were my lifeline to someone who cared, someone who knew what I had experienced. He offered me practical advice, and ensured that I did not feel alone, even as he sought to understand the context of my situation and alert the UN Security Council. Contact, empathy, compassion, shared knowledge—surely these are the cornerstones of any community.

Over the course of those four terrifying days, his daily "one minute" phone call reassured me that despite the distance, despite terrible situations and impossible commitments, human beings will persist in reaching out, in building connections, in recognizing the extraordinary gifts of others. This persistence is, in my view, the antidote to cynicism, impatience, and selfishness.

Our ability to communicate has changed enormously over the past two decades. Even as we embrace the notion of a "global village," Facebook and other trademarks have symbolized our efficiency, our smart technology, and our need to avoid too much depth and contact in order to quickly exchange information. From the world of the personal touch, we have withdrawn increasingly into ourselves, in favor of expediency, in fear of human intimacy and contact. This is not an overstatement: an international aid worker of my acquaintance recently asked me whether it was appropriate to sit and talk with a South Sudanese.

Kevin's next call found me on the floor of the Comboni Missionaries in Juba, trapped by a second volley of gunfire. I was with half a dozen other international missionaries, and all of us lay facedown on the floor as more machine gun rounds, tank shells, and rocket-propelled grenades crisscrossed our compound—this time apparently in a celebratory mood. I tried to balance my bowl of soup and listen to Kevin's faraway voice on the phone. The minute was an hour, his words—whatever he said, I cannot recall now—were comfort and solidarity, filling my bruised and bewildered body with hope. Even after he ended the call, that "one minute" continue to comfort me, to reassure me that I was alive and loved, no matter what happened tomorrow.

The art of community is not a whirlwind of actions, reports, and speeches; it is the intimacy of gestures, of words that touch and reach, and bridge the great gulf of hissing static. The global village is a mirage unless we fill it with this sense of intimacy. Kevin's call, and the calls I received from his son, Brendan, and from family and friends, taught me that there is no replacement for love, support, and true friendship.

In the winter of 2002, I returned to my hometown, Geneva, as a stranger in a familiar land. I had entered into a new phase of my life: still lacking confidence in my skills as a humanitarian, and shaken by the raw violence I saw while stationed in the Nuba Mountains of Sudan, I arrived at IDHA 9. Unbeknownst to me, this would become a defining moment in my life. Not only did I walk away from the IDHA with the professional skills and tools I needed, but I also formed friendships with people who spoke the "aid language," and who approached their work with spirit, enthusiasm, and genuine curiosity. Surrounded by so many like-minded people, I thought I had joined the IDHA in an exceptionally vintage year, or else the course had filled some niche in the humanitarian community.

From the hotel sauna to the small restaurants around Cornavin station, in clusters ever more intense and committed, friendships bloomed and strategies developed—bonds that, in many cases, remain unbreakable, connecting us across borders and oceans, coming together and forming actions, studies, shared analyses, and reunions in the most unexpected of places.

What struck me about the IDHA was the total absence of a vainglorious, step-over-one-another culture of seeking advantage and prestige; instead, there was a deep-seated sense of respect and community, reinforced through the kind of honest, open reflection that inspires confidence, in spite of our faults and fears of inadequacy. I thought perhaps I had lucked into IDHA 9, but as I pursued the MIHA—attending courses in Barcelona, New York, and Berlin, all at times of my choosing, thanks to the flexibility of the program—I came to realize that Fordham and the IIHA had tapped into a critical need in the humanitarian world, and had met that need head-on, with innovation and first-class staff and support teams.

When I arrived in Geneva for IDHA 9, I immediately felt at home. Our experiences were not only good fodder for dinner stories, but also formed the backbone of the coursework, which requires all the students to share and reflect. For many of us, it was the first time we had been afforded a chance to think about our personal experiences within the international framework, and to consider the experiences of others who were placed in similar situations. There was no competition, only support and encouragement—an educational approach that held value for both students and tutors.

The habit of reflection is no longer a luxury for armchair philosophers or would-be aid workers; it has become a tool for hundreds of humanitarians who desperately needed to process how their work has changed them, for better or for worse. Equally as important, it forces us to challenge our own narrow perceptions of an industry that at times seems to forget the moral heart of the matter and become bloated with its success.

Some believe that training for real-life emergencies is the key to humanitarian aid, but I would argue our own instincts prepare us for most situations we will face, long before the fateful day that the guns roar or the car is hijacked. I am deeply concerned that we have allowed others, who work far from the fields of emergency, to establish humanitarian policy and approaches. At the crucial juncture of experience and theory is the core of a new philosophy, a call not merely for internal reforms, but for a revolution, a repositioning, a rebirth of ideas, and a renewed sense of self and other in this bleeding world.

As an IDHA alumnus, I have a responsibility to develop this new philosophy and answer the hard questions. I now have the ability to look honestly at my life and my choices; to avoid the generalizations, the preferred political narratives, and the simplifications that stymy our efforts. The IDHA, above all, allows its students to think creatively in a field that adheres to tradition and often refuses change. In the end, the hours of reading and reflection created a space in my mind where I can question and challenge, and find myself anew.

Jesper Lund IDHA 11

I joined UNOCHA in 1999 after serving for several years in the Danish Emergency Management Agency. I felt reasonably prepared for the field, as I had led overseas operations for the agency on several occasions. The most memorable of these deployments played out over six months in the winter of 1992 to 1993, while I led convoy operations in Central Bosnia. The working conditions were extremely difficult and dangerous. I led a team of 30 former conscripts, who had been deployed to handle 20 small Mercedes trucks. Together with local mechanics, translators, and operatives, we kept the humanitarian supply chain in central Bosnia rolling.

After a few busy and eventful years, I sensed that I had reached a crossroads in my career. I was unsure whether to return to Denmark and resume my work, or resolutely pursue a future in the international humanitarian system. By chance, I came across the IDHA. The course presented the perfect opportunity to explore the humanitarian profession and reflect on my future career path. Over the course of four weeks, I would not only complete an academically recognized program, but I would also have the occasion to dive into and discuss aspects of the humanitarian system with my peers.

It was with the usual excitement—as well as trepidation in the face of the unknown—that I entered the conference room at the International Conference Centre of Geneva as a participant in IDHA 11 in late January 2003. Our cohort of around 60 students would not be disappointed: our first speaker was no other than the former UN Secretary-General, Mr. Boutros Boutros-Ghali, followed by Larry Hollingworth, who delivered an emotional presentation, and made us all feel as though we were about to undertake the most important endeavor of our lives.

The IDHA classes I attended took place on the Geneva University campus. The official atmosphere was a constant reminder of the importance of the tests we would take at the end of the course. Work in the syndicates was intense, and we studied hard to complete our assignments. Prior to the course, I had planned to spend only a handful of evenings with my group and return home most evenings; in practice, I only managed to spend one weekend at home during the entire course. Every evening we worked until after midnight.

When not preparing syndicate presentations, we were discussing humanitarian response and global politics. As friendships developed over the four weeks, we became more and more attentive and supportive of each other. The goal was no longer limited to passing the final exams; it expanded to ensuring that all the other members of our syndicate also passed.

The course coincided with an influx of international news reports on the US-led intervention in Iraq. Conversation on the daily bus ride to and from the university, and during coffee breaks, revolved around the planned intervention and the UN-mandated resolution. We were 60 students from diverse backgrounds, with diverse opinions; my class-mates included US military personnel and an Iraqi social worker; an MSF staff member who questioned the legality of the intervention; and African development workers who feared that US engagement in Iraq would divert funds away from essential programs in other countries.

Geneva is an excellent location for the IDHA program; the city is the "humanitarian capital" of the world, with hundreds of international organizations represented. However, it would be a mistake to assume that Geneva-based humanitarians spend most of their time in endless discussions with humanitarian agencies; in fact, very little time is spent meeting with colleagues from other agencies. When we do meet, it is more often to state our respective mandates and ensure that fellow humanitarian agencies do not infringe on our "territory." In the nearly four years I spent in Geneva, I hardly ever visited the offices of other humanitarian organizations. Ironically, I visited more of my peer orga-nizations as an IDHA participant than as a humanitarian professional.

As an IDHA student, I had the opportunity to observe how organiza-tions and their staff introduced themselves. These short interactions helped shape my views on the capacity and professionalism of various humanitarian actors. Now, more than a decade later, I can still recall which senior representatives seemed well prepared and proud of their work, and which did not.

Most of all, I recall the rich diversity of opinions among the IDHA students. In our syndicates, we would discuss the assigned topics for hours on end without reaching a consensus—which was perhaps the point of the exercise. As humanitarians, it is essential that we remain open to different perspectives, and that we respect one another, even if we cannot agree on a common approach. Before I joined OCHA, I was the product of a rather protected, mono-cultural environment, and I found it fascinating to hear the views of colleagues who had lived in conflict areas or in places affected by natural disaster. I had focused on technical and operational activities. Now I was suddenly introduced to a different vision, which placed beneficiaries at the center of our work and broached the eternally thorny dilemma of the transition period that follows the departure of emergency responders.

After I completed the IDHA, I joined a number of large-scale OCHA missions in Iran, Indonesia, and Pakistan. During these missions, I made good use of the knowledge I had gained from the course, and I was thankful that I had a network of IDHA friends to lean on. Social media applications had not yet evolved, and so it was more difficult to connect with and hear from each other. It became a reflex when deploying to a new emergency to send a message to IDHA 11 classmates to check whether any of them were already on the ground, or on the way to contribute to the response. Similarly, I frequently reached out to the other graduates, especially members of my syndicate group, to seek advice and guidance when facing new challenges. One should not underestimate the value of cross-organizational networks, particularly when working for an organization with a mandate to ensure effective coordination on the ground.

Today, with the help of social media platforms, communication between IDHA students has become so much easier. The ability to connect and confer across organizations is conducive to a holistic and well-coordinated response. Certainly the IDHA network has the potential to plan and play an even more important and proactive role than is the currently the case.

Speaking for myself, the IDHA course was the first step toward completing a graduate-level education. Back in 2003, the MIHA did not exist. Encouraged by my IDHA experience, I kept searching for a relevant program. By chance, Copenhagen University contacted me when they were looking for resource persons to lecture at a summer course on water management in emergencies. The course in question later developed into the Master's in Disaster Management at Copenhagen University. I completed the program with the sole objective of gaining a Master's Degree in order to pursue a career within the UN humanitarian system.

When I joined IDHA 11, the course was presented as a "driver's license" for humanitarian response. At the time, there were no alternatives to the course, nor were there any academic institutes where one could obtain a recognized certificate to work in emergency response. Today, it seems as if any self-respecting university offers some type of post-graduate degree in humanitarian response. In light of the proliferation of academic training in humanitarian response, you may well ask if there is still a need for the IDHA program. I have a straightforward answer to that question: the IDHA is the only program that places people to be assisted and those assisting them firmly at the core of the training. Larry and the entire CIHC team, who set not just the curriculum but also the tone of the course, are outstanding models for people entering the profession—a fact all the laureates of the first 50 IDHA courses can readily confirm.

International humanitarian organizations increasingly rely on national staff to implement their programs. This is great news. We need to do much more to provide national staff with basic training in the humanitarian system as many of them have limited understanding of international response mechanisms and lack basic understanding of the humanitarian principles underpinning the work of humanitarian agencies. IDHA could provide the perfect platform, in an appropriate setting and for a manageable length of time, for expanded national staff training. In the long term the challenge is to persuade both international and governmental organizations to invest in this scheme and, therefore, in their own national staff.

Sadly, I note that several years of working in humanitarian operations have shown me that daily life as a humanitarian responder often conflicts with the principles we preach when framing our interventions. Far too often we are hemmed in by organizational mandates and priorities. With technological progress, we find ourselves more and more in a "headquarters straight jacket," operating in an environment where there is no room for error; less and less are we guided by duty of care, cross-organizational exchanges, and placing beneficiaries at the heart of our work.

I clearly remember the personal approach of the IDHA, which has carried into the actions of its alumni, and our subsequent interactions with members and managers of the program. Larry and the IDHA team ensure that all students and staff feel appreciated and that their contribution is invaluable; this defines and sets the IDHA apart as a model that all humanitarian organizations would do well to imitate.

Mark Honnoraty IDHA 45

"XO, WEO Wireless Office." The electronic voice coming over the Tannoy system awoke me from a fitful sleep, and I crossed the short distance from the captain's cabin to the nerve center of the submarine, the Control Room. My Executive Officer, my second-in-command, and the Weapons Engineering Officer would ensure that we had received a verifiable signal from the Prime Minister, via our controlling headquarters in London, authorizing the release of nuclear weapons in defense of the United Kingdom and Europe.

Deep beneath the hostile waters of the North Atlantic, that was never going to be much leeway between safe and unsafe. I commanded one of the UK's four Trident Ballistic Missile submarines, and this firing drill had been repeated at least twice a week for the past 48 years to test the resolve of the crew and the efficiency of the weapon system, a cornerstone of the UK defense policy. A legacy of the Cold War, nuclear deterrence is clinical, precise, and a last resort, far removed from the realities of conflict affecting millions of people across the world.

In 2011, I was sent to Afghanistan to work on the staff of General Petraeus at the International Security Assistance Force headquarters in Kabul; a landlocked country and the perfect job for a seasoned submariner. As Chief of Integrated Operations within the Directorate of Strategic Communications, my role was to prevent fratricide between the strategic communications released within Afghanistan in support of the civil-military campaign. Working alongside the embassies of all contributing nation states, the government of the Islamic Republic of Afghanistan, and supporting intergovernmental organizations (IGOs) and NGOs, my role was to ensure that a unified voice resonated through the official communications strategy from all actors supporting the stabilization operations. For the first time in my 37-year career, I came face-to-face with the realities and human cost of conflict.

Very early on in my seven-month deployment, it became apparent that my lack of training and knowledge was offset by my companions working in the humanitarian sector. Their understanding and commitment to the people of Afghanistan was in stark contrast to the military approach of operational planning and quick wins to support a good report for promotion after a short operational tour.

My encounter with the United Nations Assistance Mission in Afghanistan and humanitarians working for The International Security Assistance Force had a profound effect on my outlook on war and conflict. Here were people, with years of experience, trying their best to make a real difference to the people of Afghanistan in contrast with the minimal experience of most military personnel when dealing with the complexities of suffering, communities, and culture.

With retirement just over the horizon, I rejected firm offers of employment form the defense industrial sector in support of the multi-billion-pound project to replace Trident submarines, and decided instead to work in the not-for-profit sector, preferably supporting victims of war and conflict.

I had plenty of crisis management and the ability to work under pressure, but I lacked an understanding of the causes of conflict and the role of the humanitarian. Before I presented myself for employment within the third sector, I know I had to address both of these shortcomings.

Despite not having a first degree, I was welcomed to IDHA 45 in June 2015. A pleasant month of sightseeing and relaxing in New York City beckoned, but I underestimated the challenge of my learning and the pace of the teaching. IDHA was as much professionally rewarding as it was personally rewarding. It radically altered my preconceived ideas and understanding of humanitarians as I came to understand the unique professional and personal challenges that my fellow students faced daily in support of their organizations. The personal experience of the teaching staff was critical in providing a novice like myself with an in-depth comprehension of the challenges that I may face in my chosen second career. As much as I admire my superior officers in the military, these humanitarians, many almost half my age, earned my respect, reinforcing my decision to join their ranks and became a humanitarian.

Since graduating from IDHA 45, I am in the second year of my Bachelor's Degree in Politics and International Relations with Quantitative Analysis, majoring in War and Conflict, at the University of Kent in the United Kingdom. All my fellow students are 35 years my younger, but I gain inspiration from their hope and aspirations for the future. For my third and final year, I have chosen two of my eight modules to further my understanding of the plight of refugees in the UK, including a work placement with Migrant Help, a UK national charity helping refugees and migrants, and a research dissertation. Using quantitative methods, I will analyze the effectiveness of government policies to assimilate Syrian refugees into local communities and assess best practice on behalf of Migrant Help. My dissertation, based on the theme of lost innocence, aims to research the changing public attitude in the UK toward child refugees and the implications of that change on national government policy. The inspiration for these modules stems from my participation in IDHA 45, where I was exposed to the work of my teachers and fellow students.

Graduating in the summer of 2018, I face the daunting prospect of presenting myself to the job market for the first time since 1978. My hope is that the combination of my military career and higher education, gained since I retired from the Royal Navy, will assist me with my ambition of working with refugees and IDPs. Putting into practice my managerial experience and newfound understanding of war and conflict, I hope to emulate the good work of my fellow students and the IDHA staff in joining their ranks.

Naomi Gikonyo   IDHA 29

I grew up in an average middle-class family in the sleepy town of Nyeri, about two hours from Nairobi, on a farm nestled in the foothills of the Aberdare Ranges. I never set out to be an aid worker; I stumbled into it by sheer luck, after securing an internship with International Medical Corps (IMC) while in my third year at the University of Nairobi. Soon after I graduated, I was offered a job as a Logistics Assistant for IMC in their Somalia office, based in Nairobi.

The "assistant" in that particular job title was perhaps a bit of a misnomer, as I found myself taking over day-to-day logistical operations when the Logistics Officer left for maternity leave less than a week after I started.

I can't quite remember how I came across the IDHA, but once I did, I was convinced it was the ideal course to help me hone my rudimentary emergency response skills, which I acquired during the post-election crisis response in Kenya. The course fee of $5,500 was, however, almost equivalent to my annual national staff salary and seemed unattainable at the time. Luckily, a timely $2,500 scholarship from the CIHC, with the balance split between my employer and myself, enabled me to attend IDHA 29 in November 2009.

The IDHA acted as a springboard to my international humanitarian career. In my opinion, the most unique thing about the course is not only the wide breadth of experience and talent that it brings together, but also the indelible bonds it creates amongst its alumni. I am still in touch with many of the individuals I met on IDHA 29, and our paths have often crossed in different parts of the world where our respective humanitarian journeys have taken us. I have since returned as a tutor on IDHA 48, an experience that only reinforced my belief that the IDHA is still one of the best humanitarian training courses available to aid workers to date.

After a year in Haiti, I was completely burnt out and left with a deep sense of disillusionment. I was a little battered and wiser to the ways of the world, and the glossy veneer of humanitarian action had started to lose a bit of its sheen. While I still firmly believed humanitarian relief was a worthy cause, I was less sure about the operational mechanisms for response. When I reflect back on my time in Haiti, an oft-repeated IDHA axiom comes to mind: "Good intentions are not enough."

It wasn't long before I shook off those doubts and found myself in the boiling cauldron brought about by the Arab Spring. I deployed to Benghazi in June 2011, about three months into the Libyan revolution, where IMC was setting up field hospitals to treat the war-wounded and civilians trapped in conflict zones. The first thing that struck me about Libyans was their boundless generosity. In the early stages of the crisis, they unreservedly donated food, fuel, generators, blankets, and other non-food items in a bid to help their less fortunate countrymen. Libya was also a relatively insular society at the time, and just opening up to the rest of the world after many decades as a pariah state under Gaddafi.

The novelty of humanitarian actors wore off quickly, as the role of North Atlantic Treaty Organization forces and humanitarian agencies became less clear. UN agencies and NGOs were perceived as "cleanup crews," and were expected to repair the damage wrought by these forces and pick sides between the warring parties. In my experience, the humanitarian principles of neutrality and impartiality were severely tested in Libya, and we constantly had to haggle, plead, and negotiate with local volunteer doctors and militia commanders to allow us to treat civilians and captured combatants at IMC-supported field hospitals. After nine months in Libya, I was once again left feeling disillusioned, and profoundly sad that the aspirations that so many Libyans had held for the revolution never materialized. It remains a country at war with itself and arguably a lot worse off than we found it.

I have worked in other field operations, as well as with the WFP at their headquarters in Rome, where I focused on emergency preparedness and broader disaster risk reduction strategies. It's been an interesting journey, to say the least, and I expect the best is yet to come. For all those who aspire to work as humanitarians, take heart, because despite all the highs and lows, the journey is worth it.

Roger Mburente   IDHA 6

I was born in the hills of Mugera, the second Catholic parish in Burundi. African missionaries founded Mugera at the end of the nineteenth century, around the time of the arrival of the Germans.

In 1972, I was 17 years old and part of the Minor Seminary of Mugera. That year, more than 300,000 Hutu, mainly from the educated class, were killed. By the grace of God, I managed to flee the violence, and eventually arrived at the refugee camp of Rilima, in southern Rwanda, some 20 miles from the border with Burundi.

I spent one year in the camp, from October 1972 to September 1973. It was the worst period of my life. There was no shelter; we had to build our own hut, without any instructions or materials. Caritas, a Catholic relief organization, delivered food supplies to the camp, but large quantities were stolen and sold in the Nyamata and Kigali markets. Some days we had nothing at all.

There were no formal water facilities. We washed ourselves in a nearby lake, and took water for cooking and drinking. Many of my companions died of waterborne diseases, malaria, and various other illnesses, due to lack of hygiene.

Where were the UN agencies? During the year I spent in Rilima, I never saw them. I saw delegates of the ICRC, members of Caritas, and representatives of the Catholic Church in Burundi, most notably the Archbishop of Kabgayi-Kigali, who visited the camp every week.

From 1973 to 1975, I attended the Saint-Paul Seminary in Kigali, a high school of the Archdiocese of Kabgayi-Kigali. It was my first chance, my first opportunity, to escape the hand I had been dealt. Many of the young people in the camp had no such opportunity to join a school. The UNHCR delegation in Rwanda, which had recently opened, paid for my school fees. UNHCR did its best to protect Burundian refugees, despite the enormous challenges local and international aid groups faced in Rwanda. I owe them a great deal for their assistance and support. In late 1975, I entered the National University of Rwanda in Butare, where I would spend the next five years. UNHCR again offered me a scholarship to complete both my Bachelor's and Master's Degrees.

After I completed my studies at the National University of Rwanda, I worked as a teacher at a Catholic high school in Butare. I was chosen to assist the French Director, since I "understood the culture," as he used to say. I held a prominent position at the school, and both staff and students respected my point of view. I spent a lot of time with the students, and happily took on the task of organizing daily classes, teachings, and religious activities.

I worked at the school for three years before I moved to Rwesero and joined the staff of another Catholic high school. The bishop asked that I teach French and accompany the students, as I had in Butare.

While I was teaching in Rwesero, I had the idea to build a high school for young Burundian refugees who did not have the opportunity to study in official schools. With help from friends and colleagues in Kigali, and with assistance from UNHCR and the Catholic Church, I was able to turn my idea into a reality. The school was built in Muvumba, in the northeast of Rwanda, where most of the Burundian refugees were relocated after the border between the two countries shifted in 1973. The school kept its doors open until 1992, when we lost many students and staff.

After five years of teaching, I left Rwanda in October 1985 to study theology in Switzerland. The bishop of Kabgayi offered me the chance to study at the University of Fribourg, and earn a Master of Theology in service of his diocese. When I completed my theological studies, I wanted to return to Africa, but the Rwandan Civil War broke out in 1990, and I was forced to remain in Europe for my own safety.

I was appointed to a parish in La Chaux-de-Fonds in the canton of Neuchâtel, where I was involved in youth activities. It was the first time that I felt happy in Switzerland, and I continue to work for the parishes in the dioceses of Lausanne, Geneva, and Fribourg. The ecumenical Taizé Community in Burgundy, France has been a great comfort to me; I spend several days on retreat in Burgundy every year, surrounded by many people who share a similar purpose.

Young people in La Chaux-de-Fonds, curious about the war and the genocide in Rwanda, asked me a great number of questions about life in Africa. They wanted an explanation for the tragedies in the African

Great Lakes region, and while I answered their questions as best I could, my answers alone were not sufficient. Some asked me to organize a visit to Rwanda and Burundi, but I dissuaded them from travel to the region. If I returned to Rwanda or Burundi, I would put myself in grave danger, but I did not have the heart to tell the members of these youth groups, who were so hopeful for change, about the reality of my situation.

In 2000, a friend of mine told me about the IDHA course. At first, I believed it would be too complicated to attend; I wanted to participate, but my English was poor, and I feared I would not be able to follow the lectures. Eventually, I decided to send my application to Michel Veuthey, and some days later, I received a call from Larry Hollingworth. Both encouraged me to attend IDHA 6 at Hunter College in New York. I took a month off work and paid for the course with my own funds; no one in the parish was able to understand what this project was about.

The course was a rich experience. The IDHA is a place where students of different backgrounds and nationalities learn to live and to work together. I immediately recognized the value of this model, which simulates the conditions in the field, where workers from different organizations and countries must come together to achieve a common goal. Wonderful!

The other students on the course wanted to know a lot about my life as a Burundian refugee in Rwanda. They also wanted to know why a parish priest would be interested in the IDHA. I answered all of these questions in French, which someone then translated into English, and as we talked and shared our experiences, I felt right at home. The IDHA quickly became my family.

When the administrators later asked if I would be a tutor on future IDHA courses, I accepted at once. It was an honor, even if I knew that it would not always be easy to teach people from different backgrounds and nationalities.

I worked closely with my assigned syndicate, and I offered advice about how to collaborate effectively. I always asked each of my students the same question: "How are you doing in the syndicate group?" I wanted to ensure that everyone had a place in the group, and I knew I was personally responsible for the welfare of the group and its members.

Teamwork is difficult. I met participants from large organizations with extensive field experience who thought they had all the answers, and didn't understand why they had to work in a syndicate. I would take these students aside, and after some long discussions and several days of adjusting to the group dynamic, they would often realize the benefits of teamwork in humanitarian response.

I tutored many syndicates with pleasure and success, and never had reason to complain about my students. On rare occasions, Larry has asked me to intervene in other groups or offer my support in difficult cases.

I respect, and am respected by, each member of the IDHA family. I have made many good friends through the IDHA, and my faith has always helped me in this endeavor; my adherence to the Catholic Church has never been a problem with the participants.

I like to teach IDHA students to question the mechanics of governance and community participation. I will often use examples from my own life to complement and inform the course lectures.

When humanitarian workers are posted in a country, we arrive with good intentions. We are fully briefed, but once we enter the field, the reality is quite different from what we learn in textbooks; the lessons are put in context, I like to say.

We must recognize that we are foreigners, and that we don't know or understand everything in the host country. Our attitudes, our way of thinking and doing, may come from a place of deep compassion, but without the involvement of local staff and the beneficiaries of our aid, therein lies the danger! Not to mention the politics, the clash of cultures, the different religions—all of which can turn fragile, complicated situations into intractable problems.

We should observe and listen in order to organize a response. We should take into account the organization and the needs of the local people. We must understand our potential political impact on the situation. Where do we stand? What kind of problems will we meet? How will we respond? Can we be neutral, impartial, and independent?

The IDHA has opened my mind. I use what I learned from the course in both my activities with local communities in developing countries, and with the young people of Switzerland, who come to me when they want to offer their time, energy, and knowledge to people in need.

In 2002, a group of people founded the Association Villageoise d'Entraide et de Développement, with the aim of improving the conditions of health and sanitation for disadvantaged people in Burundi. Many communities lacked potable water, and with the knowledge I obtained from the IDHA, the Association brought water to 5,000 people in the hills of Mugera who, until that point, had to travel for miles to collect unclean, contaminated water. The beneficiaries of the project helped dig trenches where the water pipes passed, and after the construction of the trenches, they were trained to manage and maintain the project.

We not only train local communities to construct water facilities, but also encourage these communities to obtain the materials and transportation resources for the project. We also raise funds in Switzerland to purchase materials that are not available in the regions where we work.

After the project ended, the beneficiaries were asked to elect a water committee and collect a small amount of money every month in order to maintain the construction. This kind of "exit strategy" ensures the project remains effective and self-sustainable.

The charity now supports a WASH training center that serves schools, parishes, and communes. It works very well, due in part to the skills and funding of my friends and myself.

I have recommended a number of candidates to the IDHA over the years, and all of them continue to serve their countries and their people. I am especially proud of those who run our field projects, Nestor Mburente and Leopold Simbakiye, and of Alphonse Baranshaka, who directs the agricultural work. I would also like to mention Marc Rwabahungu, the Administrative General Secretary of the Assembly of

Burundi; Espérance Uwimana, the first Counselor of the Burundian Embassy in Turkey; and Philippe Minani, the second Counselor at the Burundian Embassy in Geneva. Many African students who are alumni of the IDHA occupy senior positions in the UN system, in the international NGO community, or in the governments of their own countries. The IDHA has also helped open the eyes of the young people I teach in Switzerland to the realities of the world. In every parish I visit, I emphasize reflection on the relationships between countries, on the cooperation between the Global North and the Global North, and on the roles these actors play in emergency situations.

I'm often invited to give lectures in high schools when a new crisis occurs in the world. The lectures are often such a success that some students ask me to organize activities within the countries, which I will do, on the condition that we do not intervene in dangerous situations. I ask local communities in Africa or South America to build a proposal that will allow Swiss youth groups to work with local youth groups. Since 2000, more than 250 young people from Switzerland have traveled to work and learn in the Global South, to countries as diverse as Burkina Faso, Bolivia, Colombia, Cameroon, Burundi, Nepal, and Mexico. Most travel in groups with me for one month, others participate in homestays for a longer period. All and all, it is an excellent way to discover and understand others cultures, and to participate in local projects!

I would like to express my gratitude toward Dr. Kevin Cahill, Larry Hollingworth, Brendan Cahill, and Michel Veuthey for their humanity, and many thanks to all the students and syndicates with which I have worked. I am grateful for the opportunity that the IDHA presents to African humanitarian leaders; the course has introduced a new approach to humanitarian action, and I am proud to be an ambassador of the IDHA.

Cynthia Coffman   IDHA 47

I joined the humanitarian community in 2010, as a field administrator for MSF in post-earthquake Haiti. The previous year, I had taken three courses with RedR Australia, but I lacked hands-on experience in the field; needless to say, the six months I spent in Haiti offered me a crash course in humanitarian relief, and I enjoyed every minute of it. I went on to join five more missions in as many years. My career has taken me to Nigeria, Jordan, Iraq, the Democratic Republic of the Congo, and most recently, the southern border of Turkey.

Over the course of those five missions, I took part in countless humanitarian courses and training seminars, but I still felt that I lacked technical expertise. I realized that I wanted to study the principles, values, and history of the humanitarian field on a deeper level, and better understand how I fit into the broad spectrum of actors involved in crisis situations.

In 2015, I decided to take the next step, and I started to search for a postgraduate program that would teach me the tools and resources I needed to perform to the best of my abilities. At the time, I was stationed in Ganziantep, Turkey, where I witnessed the horrors of the Syrian conflict on a daily basis. I spent a year in Ganziantep, but the magnitude of the suffering took its toll on me, and by the end of the mission, I was ready to leave the field and return to the classroom.

I initially consulted my colleagues for advice and opinions on potential humanitarian academic programs, but I didn't have much luck. Eventually I turned to the Internet for help, and my research led me to the MIHA. As I read over the curriculum, I knew that I had found the right program for me. In addition to the rigorous academic standards and an exceptionally qualified staff, the course offered the opportunity to reflect on my role in the humanitarian community. Before I could apply to the program, I first had to complete the IDHA. I enrolled without hesitation, certain that the course would prove both relevant and necessary.

IDHA 47 far surpassed my expectations. The quality of the lectures—and the caliber of our teachers, tutors, and administrators—took me by surprise. Our lecturers spoke openly about their experiences, patiently answered our questions, and encouraged debate and discussion. I felt privileged to be in the company of humanitarians who remain so passionate about their work, even after decades in the field. Their optimistic realism, their joys and upsets, their values and principles, inspired me. It is clear that the IDHA chooses its tutors and guest speakers not only for their extensive experience and knowledge, but also for their enthusiasm and commitment to humanitarian work.

Our teachers confronted the faults and failures of the humanitarian system head-on, even as they stressed the importance of resilience and determination when faced with difficult problems. All the IDHA staff members, from professors and tutors, to guest speakers and administrators, invested an enormous amount of time and energy in the course, and it showed. Despite the long hours, fast pace, and heavy workload, the month flew by, thanks to their endless enthusiasm, flexibility, and encouragement.

I am especially thankful to my tutor, Theo Kreuzen, whose support and feedback proved invaluable. He had an excellent sense of when to help, and when to step back and let us work out the various scenarios and presentations on our own. He was an effective, passionate, and dedicated tutor, and it was apparent whenever he told stories about his time in the field, how deeply certain missions affected him. In spite of his personal sacrifice, in spite of heartbreak, he remained positive, kind, and generous with his time.

As for my peers, I appreciated the cultural and professional diversity of the IDHA student body. International aid workers sat beside military and police officers, which ensured a lively debate and a plurality of perspectives. I appreciated the opportunity to share my point of view, and never felt that I had to temper what I said. The IDHA provides a safe environment to discuss, listen, and learn. I enjoyed the frank conversations, the openness and the humor, and the fact that our teachers welcomed everyone's viewpoints, no matter how unconventional. I have the sense that the Course Administrators select students in order to create an environment where classroom discussions naturally involve different perspectives and opinions.

In addition to class discussions, the team building exercises led by Pamela Lupton-Bowers enabled the students to bond quickly with the professors, tutors, and each other. These exercises created a positive and energetic educational environment, and taught us how to communicate and collaborate effectively.

The IDHA course material was relevant, practical, thought provoking, and informative. In the field, I often had limited contact with other humanitarian agencies and missions. As an IDHA student, I learned about the history of humanitarianism, international humanitarian law, the UN system, and various cluster sectors to which I had never been exposed, such as camp management and education. I also benefited from modules on civil-military cooperation, migration, human trafficking, refugee response, and disaster management.

I particularly enjoyed learning about the humanitarian philosophies of Woodrow Wilson and Henry Dunant. I discovered that I fit quite comfortably in the Dunantist camp, which emphasizes neutrality, impartiality, and independence in situations that require intervention. Wilsonians, by contrast, believe the ends justify the means, and may compromise certain humanitarian values in order to deliver assistance to those in need.

I firmly believe, based on my field experience, that humanitarians, like physicians, should first aim to "do no harm." To quote Dr. Martin Luther King, Jr., "Constructive ends can never give absolute moral justification to destructive means, because in the final analysis, the end is pre-existent in the means." Thanks to the IDHA, I now understand the complexities and considerations that shape the Wilsonian school of thought, and I have come to realize that in certain situations, the Dunantist value system may work better in theory than in practice.

The quality of the course professors, tutors, guest lecturers, and administrators is a testament to the continued importance of the IDHA. It was a pleasure to take part in IDHA 47 and hear Mr. Elhadj As Sy, the Secretary General of IFRC, deliver our commencement speech.

After I completed IDHA 47 in February 2016, I enrolled in the MIHA. The fact that both IDHA and MIHA hold courses overseas immediately appealed to me; as a student, I've had the chance to travel to a number of countries, and learn from humanitarian professionals around the world. I've also enjoyed the company of Larry Hollingworth and Tony Land on these sojourns, both of whom help ease the transition from location to location. Thus far, I've completed all but one of the MIHA courses. I've also completed three intensive Arabic courses in Amman, Jordan, and I've decided to pursue field opportunities in the region, once I receive my diploma. I can confidently say that without the IDHA and the MIHA, I wouldn't feel nearly as qualified or prepared to pursue humanitarian work in the Middle East.

I am indebted to Fordham and the IIHA not only from an academic standpoint, but also in terms of the personal and professional opportunities these programs have afforded me. As a member of the IDHA family, I now have access to a vast network of contacts in the field. Recently, I enjoyed a dinner in Amman with several graduates. Some of them I had never met before, but even so, we immediately bonded over on our common interests and experiences, and left the dinner as friends.

Before I enrolled in IDHA 47, I lacked a solid foundation in the history and theory of humanitarian intervention; now, I feel much more confident in my capacity as an aid worker, and I have a wide set of tools and contacts to draw on when difficult questions arise or additional resources are needed. It's impossible to have all the answers in a field as complex as humanitarian relief, where situations evolve so rapidly and involve so many actors, but as an IDHA graduate, I know what and who to consult when I'm faced with a problem I can't solve on my own.

In 1817, Thomas Jefferson wrote, "Knowledge is power, knowledge is safety, and knowledge is happiness." Thanks to the IDHA, I have exponentially expanded the limits of what I know. I've made wonderful friends, gained an extensive and valuable network of colleagues, and acquired the tools to help others as best as I can. I have learned concrete humanitarian concepts and theories, analyzed case studies, and heard the personal experiences of professors and participants. Most importantly, I've developed a clearer idea of where I fit into the humanitarian system, and of where I'd like my career to take me. While I've always had an instinctive sense of the career path I want to pursue, I can now justify the direction I've taken and the choices I've made along the way.

I am very grateful to have discovered the IDHA program. I have met wonderful people, gained an extensive and valuable network of friends and colleagues, and acquired tools that will allow me to become a better humanitarian aid worker.

I would like to extend a special thanks to Brendan Cahill, Tony Land, Larry Hollingworth, and Suzanne Arnold for their dedication and commitment to the IDHA. Their professionalism, expertise, and humanitarian spirit continue to inspire me.

Luvini Ranasinghe IDHA 35

In October 2007, I was working in Colombo, Sri Lanka for IFRC. One morning my immediate supervisor announced that he would be leaving for a month to participate in the IDHA course. I was simply speechless. What the hell is this guy doing, leaving the office for a month? Immediately I looked up the IDHA, and at first, I was a bit skeptical. The syllabus sounded very broad, and I wondered to myself how all of these topics could be condensed into a one-month curriculum. My supervisor returned to work after he completed the IDHA, and he didn't stop talking about it for days. He was full of energy and enthusiasm when he explained to us his experience. I checked the course calendar and promised myself that I would apply for the course in the coming months.

Life in the humanitarian sector unfolds in such a way that sometimes we don't have control over our calendars. I worked in different humanitarian positions in the Democratic Republic of the Congo, Haiti, and South and North Korea, before I finally applied to the IDHA course held in Kuala Lumpur. My supervisor told me that the selection process for the IDHA is highly competitive, and so it felt like a dream coming true when I received the acceptance letter to the course in the mail. I couldn't have been happier.

I flew to Malaysia with much enthusiasm. Kasia, a superb Course Administrator, welcomed me when I first stepped through the doors. The opening ceremony that evening was crisp and candid. I was still skeptical of the course, and wondered how any one person could manage such a dynamic and vibrant audience, but then I met Larry Hollingworth. Larry's welcome address was eloquent and persuasive, and I was mesmerized by his words. I couldn't wait for the course to begin the next day, simply because I would have the chance to hear him speak again.

More than 200 hours of lectures, presentations, debates, and group work lay ahead of me. Every day was different in its structure and content. Every lecture was unique and, more importantly, field-oriented.

The course provided both an academic and practical orientation to various aspects of humanitarian assistance, including negotiation, management, psychology, communications, education, international law, civil-military relations, politics, and economics.

The introductory lectures on the humanitarian landscape were extremely important, and set the tone for the rest of the course content. The lectures on human rights law, international humanitarian law, and immigration law provided me with a theoretical understanding of my profession. I specifically remember the first week of lectures were cutting edge, and made me realize that my six years in the humanitarian field was a blink of an eye compared to Larry's many years of experience working in complex situations around the world. It was obvious that I had a lot to learn, and I was content to simply listen to Larry and Tony Land talk about their experiences.

The lectures of the first week focused on team building, leadership, management, and motivation, and were well crafted to suit a wide audience of students who came from diverse backgrounds but shared a common goal. The main highlight of the first week was the syndicate presentation. We were given a topic to prepare a presentation for the end of the week. After our lectures ended for the day, we worked with our team mentor long into the night to prepare for the presentation. We were professionals from different backgrounds, different organizations, with very different working styles, who were forced to come together and talk about a single topic. We argued, disagreed, fought, came back together to discuss, argued again. We were not ready until Thursday night when we all finally came to an agreement about the format and content of our presentation.

We decided to do our presentation in the format of a TV show. We enjoyed preparing until Friday morning dawned, and we were very eager to present. It slowly became clear to me that learning to work with this team for the next three weeks was an essential component of the course. We needed to find a way to listen and collaborate more effectively, because in the midst of the crisis, there is no time for petty squabbles. The humanitarian field requires an enormous amount of teamwork and trust; the IDHA faculty is well aware of this fact, and created situations that strengthened our team's ability to communicate clearly and calmly.

I was very excited that weekend to study for the weekly test and do some research to write the academic paper. I should confess that I felt like a schoolgirl on Monday morning; I was incredibly nervous about the test, and I wanted to do my best and get all the answers right.

The second week was a major hit. The core work of the sector was perfectly condensed into lectures on shelter, planning, and construction; WASH; camp management; education; and communicable diseases. This last session was of great use to me while I served as an IFRC spokesperson in Haiti during the cholera outbreak. My theoretical knowledge about the subject helped me prepare for press briefings and interviews. Community participation in humanitarian action is at the heart of the IFRC model. In addition to the IDHA, I decided to take a short, specialized IIHA course on the subject, and what I learned in that course has proved extremely useful.

In the second week, we approached the teamwork aspect of the course more positively. We focused on the topic of our presentation, and despite a few difficulties—and some moments where we had to "agree to disagree"—we all learned to listen to the different opinions of group members and find common ground.

Case studies, especially those presented by Larry and Tony about the Daadab camp in Kenya, were extremely powerful. Their lectures gave a plethora of information related to the history of humanitarian response and how one can handle complex issues in an objective manner.

In the third week, we dove deep into crosscutting issues in the field, such as gender-based violence, children in armed conflicts, psycho-social issues, and negotiations in humanitarian response. The lecture about negotiations was particularly memorable, and I again decided to sign up for a specialized course on the subject after the IDHA ended.

The second focus of that week was project cycle management, and Tony Land proved to be the guru of this subject. We were given all necessary tools and tactics in order to manage a project, big or small, without any hesitation.

The fourth week focused on security, personal health, and other related matters we need to master in order to be successful in our respective jobs. Knowing the theory and the technicalities is not sufficient in the field; humanitarian workers must be capable of working under pressure, in volatile situations, while exposed to disease or physical threats. Larry has spent an enormous amount of time in the field, and he very humbly shares his experiences and expertise with the participants. His lectures are immensely helpful to those of us who face our own challenges when we return to work.

Around 200 hours of lectures from world-renowned humanitarian experts during one month was an absolute treat to my ever-inquisitive brain, and I concluded the IDHA with a strong desire to attend other courses offer by the IIHA. I consider myself truly blessed to have spent that month in such a vibrant classroom, and I will forever treasure the knowledge and guidance I received from Larry and his team.

My career sees me regularly swapping a suit and tie for boots, jeans, and a t-shirt; conferences centers for refugee camps, hotels for hospitals. When I am at one end of the job—working on social media strategy, or discussing trends in media and migration with journalists and aid workers—my mind is full of burnished images from the other, more tangible side of my work.

Life is full of contrasts. The humanitarian world of New York and Geneva, Nairobi and Kathmandu, which IDHA crisscrosses, is my world.

The ability to hop through states of mind and states of emergency helped me succeeded as an IDHA student at Fordham in that dismal, monsoon-like Manhattan of 2003; it helped me again as a tutor in the vastly superior summer of 2004; and it has helped me tell the human side of the Haiti earthquake, the Bay of Bengal crisis, the havoc wrought by typhoons in the Philippines and Vanuatu, and the chaos that unfolded on the border of Tunisia and Libya during the Arab Spring.

I am savoring the chance to write about two months—one year apart—of my life; two months that I go back to almost every day. I've more than one or two hat-tips to make here, but one certainly goes to Joss Gillijns, a veteran of IDHA 10. One morning as I was lurking in the corridors of the IFRC headquarters in Geneva, I spotted the wiry Belgian and remarked that I hadn't seen him around much. He told me he'd been over in New York, studying humanitarian affairs.

Studying humanitarian affairs? When I returned from a harrowing white-knuckle first mission in Somalia and Sudan in 1993, I was determined to educate myself about the "aid business," and duly filled out an IDHA application form. Once I received the acceptance letter, I brought the good news to Pamela Lupton Bowers and Harold Masterson in the IFRC training department.

Thus it came to pass that I checked into Fordham in early June 2003 for a month of, well, I wasn't sure what, really. I do remember being nonplussed at the start. I was 38 at the time, far too old to be a callow youth, and old enough to have a little more humility. Now that I have punched through more than half a century, I can see a little more clearly. If you want to learn about JavaScript or SEO or the Algorithm (whatever those are), then look for a hipster with an interesting neck tattoo and impeccable taste in bagels. If it's wisdom you're after, if you want to *learn*, then listen to those with experience, especially those whose names start and end with honorifics. I got over myself pretty fast, probably much more to do with expert handlers on the course than any instinctive reality check. Within days I was—the image has just popped into my mind—like a fiery colt in a field, and Larry and Dr. Cahill, the seasoned gauchos who saw some potential, who set out to stretch me, who had cool water and hay at the end of the day.

Another "Joe Knows Best" moment happened at the first meeting of our study group, and again, I cringe at the memory. We'd been unable to fix a time to meet, so I went to look for refreshments. A couple of hours later, I sashayed back into our living quarters to find a meeting of said study group in full swing. Without me! The nerve!

I lost contact with all my peers from 2003 (translation for anyone born after 1998: I'm not friends with them on Facebook). This was all in the distant past, of course, in the days when if you wanted to contact someone, you had to send an email. I imagine that every IDHA intake post-2007 has its own Facebook group, and that you busily share birthday greetings, thoughts on the migrant crisis, and pictures of pains au chocolat that look like sloths.

But there was one fellow student I remember really well, and with whom I regret not keeping in touch. He was a military man, young, tough, and blond, and as I recall he went into the army from foster care, to get an education and avoid what he saw as the inevitable slide into gang life, prison, and an early grave. He was possibly the smartest person I have ever met, able to succinctly form and express an opinion based on extensive reading coupled with growing up in the school of hard knocks.

One day, as I was boring the lecture hall with some monologue or other from my seat, I noticed he was looking at me with an expression on his face that I realized, in a stunned way, was approbation.

It was a quiet eureka moment. I realized that I had an opinion.

I've always been able to write, to talk, to communicate (well, not always, but since my voice broke, and I stopped blushing whenever I spoke to girls). But this was different. In Somalia and Sudan and Liberia in the 1990s, at the UN Headquarters in Geneva, even as I got to know the role better on postings to Georgia and Russia, I was always in awe of those with profound insights on humanitarianism, people could read current affairs—or the local war—like chess grand masters. I always felt a bit inadequate around these people and took refuge in being a smartarse, or telling jokes that shifted the attention back to me and away from any subject I felt exposed on.

IDHA gave me a valuable breather from doing the work, a time to sit back and look at what I had accomplished, what the humanitarian community had accomplished, what the world was doing to itself, and if we were making a blind bit of difference. It allowed me to think, rather than do, and my peers gave me an idea of my place in this vast firmament, an affirmation that I was doing what I wanted to do and possibly even doing it well.

That affirmation became a confirmation a few months later when Brendan Cahill asked me to come back to Fordham as a tutor. I bonded with Brendan and the other tutors like siblings, and there were many excellent chats late into the night. Brendan welcomed us to Fordham like favorite cousins (I'm thinking there must be several dozen of them in the extensive Cahill clan already). He wined and dined us, got us out of our summer torpor, and made it easy to slip into the laidback pace of June in the empty Upper West Side. He prepared us for the classroom, and though I say it myself, we did an excellent job and loved every minute of tutoring. Of course, Larry made it easy for us by being the leader you need, like a grandfather teaching you to ride a bicycle, a presence you know is behind you, willing you on, but ready to catch you if you fall.

Certain people put you right at ease, and make you feel like you are heard and respected. Brendan is one of those people. I must have gone to him with a hundred dopey questions that I could probably have solved for myself, but every time Brendan would look up from the screen, his notes, his phone and say, "Hey, Joe, how goes it?" and he'd natter about music, tell a yarn, arrange to meet after dinner. Brendan, like his esteemed father, *cares*. He's generous with the one thing that's most precious: his time.

One of the reasons I am so delighted to be asked to pen these reminiscences is that Brendan has constantly asked me to lecture, tutor, or write for IDHA, and I've rarely been able to say yes, due to my children and other commitments.

I suspect that others will write more about the substance of the lectures, the *raison d'être* of IDHA, but I was asked for a personal reflection, so I've let it all tumble out. IDHA was an important part of my life. It taught me to trust my instincts. It showed me that the decision I made early in my working life, to work for something other than the enrichment of a Board of Directors, was a solid one. As that wonderful humanitarian and ally of IDHA, Margareta Wahlström, told me when I was lucky enough to work for her at IFRC: "The only bottom line we have is human life."

In darker days, on my return from Somalia, I treated my mild case of post-traumatic stress disorder with Guinness and introspection. I wrote some pretty bad poems. In one, I posed a question that remained unanswered until I became an IDHA alumnus. Was any of it worthwhile? Whose bodies, souls, hearts, and minds did any of us save?

Thanks to the dozens of dedicated humanitarians I met at IDHA— students, mentors, organizers—and thanks to the flame lit by Dr. Cahill and Larry Hollingworth, a torch carried on by Brendan and his staff, that question is no longer rhetorical. We have saved many lives, and changed many souls, hearts, and minds through our actions. We don't just work for our organizations; we work for humanity, for those we serve, and for each other. Going through IDHA, be it in New York, Geneva, Nairobi, or Kathmandu, is life changing. It's not a substitute for humanitarian experience, but it's definitely a complement to it.

Nineteen years have passed since the autumn of 1998, when Idanna and I were seated in Dr. Kevin Cahill's waiting room in New York. We had just returned from Indonesia, and we were eager to be examined by Dr. Cahill, whose exceptionally keen eyes can spot even the most obscure exotic microbe. We were enjoying the memorable Irish wit of his marvelous assistant, Joan Durcan, when Kevin appeared, and warmly welcomed us into his office. As always, he began to narrate a poignant story that would leave a strong impression on both of us.

The terrible conflict in the Balkans was still fresh in our minds. Yugoslavia had been torn apart, and as a veteran of humanitarian disaster response, Dr. Cahill spoke about the new dilemma that UN agencies confronted in the region: a large number of young people from around the world had joined the refugee relief community, as had happened before in other, similar crises.

This time, however, it had become apparent that, despite their compassion and good intentions, they did not have the strength and emotional detachment needed to handle the situation in the field. Many were struck by sickness, while others were so traumatized by the effects of the war that they required as much care as the refugees. They, and many others from international NGOs, had become burdens and had to be sent home.

"The UN can no longer afford to assign field workers in crises without any experience or training," Kevin said. He then told us about the IDHA, and we can both still recall the passionate ring of his voice as he described the visionary four-week training program in detail. The IDHA was the first educational program of its kind, a course that relied on the collaborative efforts of leading experts in the complex interdisciplinary field of humanitarian aid. His description of the program immediately caught our attention, even though we had never worked in crisis situations, and we voiced our interest in attending.

"We teach professionals from UNICEF, ICRC, MSF, WFP," he said, his eyes gleaming as he listed the various international organizations, agencies, and others. "However, it's important to have an interesting mix of students. Let me think about it. As writers, you may be fine additions."

Later that evening, as we mulled over what Kevin had told us, we became convinced that we had to try our utmost to participate in the IDHA. We firmly believed that the course would deepen our awareness of the world and its harsh realities, and would change our approach to life, whether or not we would ever become professional humanitarians. We reflected on all the implications and hoped against hope that the doctor would accept us—which eventually he did.

In the deep of winter, we found ourselves on the shores of Lake Geneva in the Château de Bossey, encircled by Alpine peaks. Before we plunged into the intensive, four-week retreat led by the extraordinary Larry Hollingworth, we met our colleagues: men and women who had spent most of their lives in regions of the world torn apart by violence, disaster, and famine.

Like pious medieval clergy attending a synod in Rome, these humanitarian relief workers walked among the ancient oaks of the estate, unsettled by the untouched beauty of the place. The peaceful lake stretched out before them, but in their minds were the refugee camps of Bosnia, Macedonia, Rwanda, and Sudan; the devastation of Honduras, Somalia, and Sierra Leone; the minefields of Cambodia; the civil war in Sri Lanka. Their eyes carried the look of those who had witnessed the most intractable problems of human suffering.

With these men and women we broke bread. Each day opened to a new reality as we sat next to each other, listening to experts unravel the intricacies of humanitarian assistance. From the diplomatic art of communication in conflict resolution to surviving hostage situations, from camp management to treating trauma, all was presented through the lens of personal experience. We heard stories of destruction and mayhem, and walked through labyrinths of anarchy. Yet from that darkness, rays of light shone with compassion and hope. In those shared moments, a collective awareness grew; we learned to see, feel, and understand the wounds of the world.

A month later, in Italy, another tragic story reached out and grabbed us. In Naples, the city of Idanna's grandmother, we came across a small, empty church. We ventured inside and saw, to our surprise, Caravaggio's *The Seven Acts of Mercy,* lit only by the muted sunbeams that fell through the eye of the cupola.

As we stood, admiring the huge altarpiece, a man came forward: Angelo, the guardian of this treasure. He told us with intense words of when and how this painting had struck his eyes and heart. Unexpectedly, he opened a window into the power of art to enlighten and elevate.

Escaping a death sentence in Rome, Caravaggio arrived in Naples as a fugitive, and created this painting. He offered a fresh take on the timeless works of mercy: feeding the hungry, giving water to the thirsty, sheltering the homeless, visiting the prisoner, clothing the naked, healing the sick, and burying the dead. In his radical vision, this artistic genius broke with tradition and used Neapolitans on the streets as his models, placing them in scenes that defied the religious art of his age.

As Ingrid Rowland wrote recently in the New York Book Review, "When Caravaggio shows a humble disciple or an innkeeper, he shows them as full human beings. When he shows suffering, he stands his ground rather than shrinking back."

In a city that survives on a knife-edge between cruelty and grace, these works of mercy resonate with universal meaning, as relevant today as when the artist brushed his oils onto the canvas four centuries ago.

The same passion that we felt in Bossey with our colleagues and teachers of the IDHA, we found echoing in that Caravaggio masterpiece, and in the heart of Naples. All sacred traditions speak to compassion and human solidarity, which remain the cornerstone of every faith. Their voices echo across great distances and time, chanting the same refrain.

Is it not to share your food with the hungry and to provide the poor wanderer with shelter—when you see the naked, to clothe them, and not to turn away from your own flesh and blood?

—Isaiah LVIII, 7

The Prophet said: "The captive is your brother... Since he is at your mercy, ensure that he is fed and clothed as well as you are."

—Mohammad (570–632), Hadith

Every religion has the wholesome core of love, compassion and good will. The outer shell differs, but give importance to the inner essence and there will be no quarrel. Don't condemn anything, give importance to the essence of every religion and there will be real peace and harmony."

—Ashoka (third century BC)

Tzu-kung asked:"Is there a single word which can be a guide to conduct throughout one's life?"The master said,"It is perhaps the word *shu*. Do not impose on others what you do not desire for yourself.

—Confucius (551–479 BC),The Annalects XV, 24

I was hungry and you gave me food. I was thirsty and you gave me drink. I was a stranger and you welcomed me. I was naked and you clothed me. I was sick and you visited me. I was in prison and you came to me.

—Matthew 25:35–37

In August 1999, three months later, in the northern Australian coastal city of Darwin, we boarded a UN plane headed to Dili in East Timor as part of the UN Mission to East Timor. It was our first humanitarian assistance mission. The Timorese had been called to vote on a Referendum on Indonesia's rule of their country, after 26 years of occupation following the departure of the Portuguese colonial power.

From Dili, we were transferred by helicopter to the remote mountain region of Same, under the looming peaks of Mount Kablaki. In the morning, our work with East Timorese village-volunteers began. Together, we had to prepare, register, and instruct the inhabitants for the historic vote. We made our way down a forest road lined with white flowering Arabica coffee plantations that thrived in the tropic highlands. In a dirt-floor schoolhouse with flimsy walls of bamboo strips, we met our team. Even with their cheerful humility, those young men and women knew what was at stake.

By day, lines of people flocked down the dirt paths to register at our simple schoolhouse: aged farmers, wives and husbands, illiterate mountain men, even a lame grandmother carried in on a stretcher by her sons. By night, pro-government militias launched their campaign of terror, inspired by their Indonesian military sponsors. Crackling gunshots broke the silence. We awoke in cold sweat. Across the valley, strange cries could be heard. With each new dawn, more frightened villagers filled our house, huddling in corners and seeking safe haven. As soon as the sun rose, they all quietly folded the blankets and began their day. We could smell the scent of uncertainty and fear everywhere.

After two long weeks, the fateful day of August 30 arrived. In pre-dawn darkness, Idanna and I rose quietly and crept out over sleeping bodies. When our jeep approached the schoolhouse, we saw a mass of shadows. Before us was a black sea of faces, the silhouettes of hundreds. Despite all the threats and intimidation, they had braved the night. For the first time in their lives, they were about to vote and would choose their future on a world stage. A powerful sense of human solidarity filled the air.

In total silence, we walked through the crowd and passed shadowed figures. From the schoolhouse window, we then watched how, out of respect, the sea of humanity parted for the elders. All around the perimeter of the land, we spotted Indonesian soldiers, their guns pointed towards the crowd.

All of a sudden, we recalled Caravaggio's painting: a man placed a blanket on the shoulders of an elder. A water jug was passed to a thirsty mouth. Bread was offered. A sick woman was sustained and helped into our polling station by two adolescent boys. On that day, we knew that even the dead would be honored. The spirits of their ancestors seemed to be present among the multitude of people in line.

By noon, the blazing tropic sun pounded down. The line still stretched for almost a mile. There were no arguments, no raised voices. All took place quietly and orderly. No one walked away before voting. By five in the afternoon, the line still continued to advance.

At dusk, it was over. The ballot boxes were sealed by the observers, then loaded into trucks and driven to the airstrip and lifted onto the waiting UN helicopter. The blades swirled, kicking up dust as the chopper slowly rose in the twilight sky and flew off to Dili for the official count.

As night fell, everyone sensed the outcome: a landslide for inde-pendence. Smiles swept the tiny town. The melodic sounds from a

116

wedding celebration were heard from a hilltop for miles, adding to the general euphoria. Sitting in our house, we broke bread with our hosts and listened, mesmerized, to that amazing traditional music—until the unspeakable happened.

Suddenly, the festivities went dead as gunfire echoed in the encircling hills. A young man barged through the door. His face was covered in sweat. "The militias, they've set up check-points," he cried out. "All roads out of town are blocked. No one can leave. We're trapped."

Cut off from the wide world, we huddled with our friends in the dark, all pressed in front of the television. Flickering images of rampaging militias in the capital city of Dili flashed before us. Fear suffocated the room, while across the island, Indonesian-paid gangs embarked on an orchestrated spree of violence.

In the morning, an official arrived with orders for us. "We evacuate in an hour." Meanwhile, our Timorese friends were ready for their escape into the mountains. The smell of burning wood filled the air. Homes torched by the militias were going up in flames. Those who stayed behind would face the long knives of vengeance. In the confusion, one of our hosts, Emilio, handed me a faded sepia photograph. Idanna and I stared at the portrait of a tribal chief, in his traditional regalia, eyes frozen in time.

"My grandfather, Boaventura," Emilio explained. "He led our rebellion against the Portuguese 80 years ago. Keep it safe. Now, leave." Grabbing our bags, Emilio rushed us off the porch, calling: "Don't forget us."

We arrived just as the white UN helicopter swooped down to airlift us away. The dreaded Indonesian soldiers, Kopassus, could be seen at a certain distance. We were the last foreign witnesses to leave. Now they could act with impunity.

When we flew into Dili, the streets were deserted. Plumes of black smoke climbed high into the sky, covering the horizon in grey haze. The airport was in panic as we all rushed into the last C-47 transport plane. We sat with the last UN election monitors bound for Darwin. As we took off, Idanna looked out the window towards Mount Kablaki, where our friends in Same had fled into hiding.

A week later, when the smoke finally lifted, only ruins remained. The devastation was biblical: scorched earth, rotting corpses, slaughtered livestock. All agricultural tools had been destroyed, the rich lands rendered sterile. A quarter of the population had been herded across the border into West Timor while 80 percent of the buildings in East Timor had been destroyed. Indonesia's leaders accused the Western media of distorting the truth—but even so, the vote stood, and now East Timor was a free and independent state.

Today, the benighted city of Naples, much like East Timor 15 years ago and other conflict emergency zones across the globe, are seen as living hells. The Italian writer Italo Calvino offers us a different optic with which to view these worlds. He says we must, "learn to recognize who and what, in the middle of hell, is not hell and then make them endure, give them space."

In Naples, Caravaggio was faced with a humanity he had never seen before—not in the north, where he was born, and certainly not in Rome under the merciless Pontifical rule. Yet within the incredible Neapolitan misery, the famine and disease, the disparity between the rich and poor, he found extraordinary human warmth. The works of mercy were part of daily life. Thus he portrayed a group of simple people helping one another, 16 characters drawn from the *popolo*. They do not seem aware that they are performing mercies: it is simply who they are. Caravaggio lifted these people from the profane to the sacred, and his vision remains radical, 400 years later.

Not much has changed in today's Naples. The other face of this city is miraculous and authentic, but rarely this is mentioned in the press, in books or films. Instead, one hears only the permanent echo of "mafia, garbage, violence, and poverty" —but there is a light that illuminates the darkness.

The Pio Monte della Misericordia, a medieval humanitarian institution that commissioned Caravaggio's painting, has never ceased its mission of solidarity, and it continues to offer a helping hand to Neapolitans in need. This is the spirit of the city that Caravaggio immortalized so vividly in *The Seven Acts of Mercy*.

James Joyce once wrote, "I always write about Dublin, because if I can get to the heart of Dublin, I can get to the heart of all the cities of the world. In the particular is contained the universal."

Caravaggio has taken a crowded alley in Naples and raised it to the universal. From the mundane to the mythic, Naples is today's Damascus, Calcutta, or even the Bronx.

The IDHA taught us to see and touch what was essential. In those intense, unforgettable four weeks, we were shown the neglected, passed-over parts of the world, and made participants in the seven acts. The IDHA was pivotal moment in our lives, a turning point. Thank you, Kevin, Larry, and Brendan for this enduring gift.

MHCE and MIHA

The CIHC and IIHA have organized many specialized academic courses, usually of one to two-week duration. They are scheduled in sequence to accommodate the busy schedules of students who work for relief organizations. The courses are offered in locations around the world to minimize travel costs and visa problems. Among the dozens of programs are intense tutorials in humanitarian negotiations, logistics, strategic issues, natural disasters, vulnerable populations, education in conflict, accountability, human rights, ethics, disaster management, forced negotiation, community participation, leadership and management, and more.

These courses allow candidates for the Master of Arts in Humanitarian Affairs (MIHA) at Fordham University to fulfill their credit requirement in a flexible fashion. The courses are open to European universities that are members of the Network on Humanitarian Action (NOHA). The IIHA at Fordham is the lead member of NOHA in the United States.

In addition to the IDHA, the CIHC and the IIHA provide training courses for professionals from a wide variety of fields, as cited in Larry Hollingworth's chapter (page 39). Since space does not permit an extensive coverage of all these courses, I selected two of our most frequently presented programs, Mental Health in Complex Emergencies (MHCE) and the MIHA.

The MHCE has been offered in many localities around the world. I asked Larry Hollingworth to interview Lynne Jones, with whom he co-directs MHCE, about the evolution of the course. Tony Land, spent 24 years with UNHCR, has been a teacher on many IDHA courses, and is the Academic Advisor for the MIHA. Due to his vast experience and familiarity with the program, he has contributed a separate section on the MIHA.

Lynne Jones   MHCE

(As recorded in conversation with Larry Hollingworth).

I had seen you around, Larry, in Bosnia. You were so well known, and to be honest, you have not changed a bit! We first met at an NGO forum in Sarajevo, and we spoke about our jobs and our responsibilities. Out of the blue, and to my great surprise, you said in that decisive way of yours, "I want you to come and teach on the course that we run in New York." I told you I'd be delighted to teach in New York, but you would have to pay for my expenses, since neither I, nor my agency, could. You said, "Don't worry; we'll take care of everything."

I thought no more about your offer and soon left for Majorca, where I wrote the first edition of my Bosnia book. Time passed, and I thought I would hear no more. Then I received a call from you: "I need you over here in New York to tutor on our course." So off I went!

I had wanted to participate in the IDHA myself, since the curriculum covers such an extensive range of humanitarian subjects; there's no other course like it. Now I found myself directly involved in the IDHA, and most importantly, I had a whole day to teach Mental Health in Complex Emergencies.

I met Dr. Kevin Cahill for the first time in his beautiful apartment in New York. We discussed what he wished me to do. "I am giving you a free hand. Teach what you think the participants need to know." This was very generous of him, given how little he knew about me. I felt honored, and somewhat daunted, by his trust in my abilities, but I think the first mental health day went well.

In fact, the whole month was a fantastic crash course in humanitarian work. I particularly remember being "kidnapped" on the security day at West Point. The "kidnapping" was incredibly realistic, and anyone who has spent time in insecure areas knows that this kind of security role-play is a vital component of any field-training course.

It was so much fun to be in the middle of New York, in Manhattan, a short walk to Central Park. My fellow tutors were very professional, especially Nikki, with whom I shared an accommodation. The students came from a wide variety of backgrounds, and arrived ready to learn and listen.

After the course ended, I returned to the field and heard nothing more about MHCE until Larry reached out and asked me to be part of a Conflict Resolution course at the Henry Dunant Centre in Geneva. That course was one of the best that I have ever attended, and we held it again the next year in New York. I still remember role-playing an "ugly checkpoint" procedure with Larry, and conducting the oil pricing game, which is a wonderful exercise for sharpening negotiation skills. I continue to make use of what I learned from the other tutors, and to incorporate more of these "games" that combine both psychological and political conflict resolution techniques.

I thought that course would be my final contribution to the IDHA. However, about two years later, Brendan Cahill contacted me and said, "We love your mental health bit. Why don't you do a week?" I recalled Dr. Cahill's encouragement to teach what I thought was needed, and realized that I had a truly unique opportunity to orientate people to the best approach to mental health issues *before* they went into the field. In particular, I could shift the emphasis away from post-traumatic stress disorder, which was a popular and prevalent topic in humanitarian affairs at the time, and instead offer training on other important issues that received less attention, such as methods to provide social support to people who have lost everything, and how to treat psychosis when there are no medications available and no hospitals for hundreds of miles.

Obviously I could not do this alone. IMC, where I worked at the time, realized the benefit of training both local and international staff, and kindly allowed me to use office time to arraange and run the courses. I contacted an anthropologist I had met in Afghanistan, Willem Van De Put, who worked at the time for HealthNet TPO, and I asked him to help me organize the course. His insights on the importance of culture and community helped shape the curriculum. Richard Mollica, who helped me with my Bosnian research and who ran clinics for Southeast Asian refugees in Boston, taught on our first course.

The course has also hosted a number of accomplished lecturers, many of whom take time away from their incredibly busy schedules to come and teach our students. Some of these lecturers have challenged orthodox views of mental health treatment. Paul Bolton and his team at Johns Hopkins University, for instance, have taught assessment, monitoring and evaluation, and research techniques on many of our courses, and have openly questioned the imposition and validity of Western assessment methods in collecting data in other cultures. I was also able to pursue a particular bee in my bonnet: the neglect of severe mental health disorders in the field and the need for psychiatrists in humanitarian settings.

The development of the course coincided with the formation of a task force to write the Inter-Agency Standing Committee Guidelines for Mental Health and Psychosocial Support in Emergency Settings, which was a fortunate coincidence. I had the opportunity to join that task force, and our discussions profoundly influenced my own perspective on mental health procedures in emergencies. The Guidelines have provided a structure to the course since 2007, and many members of the task force—Mike Wessells, Mark Van Ommeren, Amanda Melville, and Pieter Ventevogel—later joined our faculty.

The course has also opened the door to collaborations with new partners, some of whom found us by chance. While I was based in Kampala, Uganda, I asked a colleague from UNICEF to send students to attend our course. She was so enthusiastic about the idea that she asked us to run the course for all 40 members of the staff. Thanks to TPO Uganda, we were able to provide field training on that course, as well as mental health training. We also had the chance to run a course at the London School of Hygiene and Tropical Medicine, due to our connection to Professor Vikram Patel, whom we have been fortunate to have as a teacher in both London and Kampala.

Like the IDHA, the MHCE course travels, which allows local staff to attend. The students come from such a diversity of backgrounds and experiences, and they all have something to say and viewpoints to share. Their opinions on mental health and psychosocial support have helped shape and challenge my own notions.

The course has benefited from the strength of our alumni connections. Students often become faculty, and faculty become Course Directors. Inka Weissbecker, one of our graduates, is now the Global Mental Health Coordinator for IMC and a regular teacher on the course, which IMC continues to support; Pieter Ventevogel is a Senior Mental Health Officer at UNHCR, as well as an MHCE Course Director.

And, needless to say, we have been lucky to have you, Larry, with us almost every year.

There are three important aspects to the course. Firstly, the MHCE serves a distinct and crucial purpose in the humanitarian world. Today, there are a number of courses on global mental health, including the WHO Mental Health Gap Action Programme (mhGAP), which trains staff to work in low-income communities. While we have certainly benefited and learned from mhGAP and other similar programs, the mental health needs in crisis situations are very specific and unique, and are best addressed by experienced humanitarian professionals.

Secondly, the course brings together an unusual combination of students. Some are humanitarian workers with no prior mental health experience who want to learn what psychosocial programs are available, why they matter, and how to run them; others are mental health professionals with no field experience, who want an introduction to humanitarian work. Every course attracts students with different career goals, which leads to a rich and productive exchange of ideas and experiences. This has been particularly true in the last few years, as more and more local humanitarians—from places as far away as Syria, Nepal, Ethiopia, Palestine, and Sierra Leone—have started to attend the MHCE. Our students offer such a wealth of experiences that in the past two courses, we have dedicated half a day to hearing their programming ideas.

Thirdly, the course has a broad agenda. We always try to include local tutors, and we provide lessons on sensitive subjects like sexual violence, child protection, and security. Some students ask, "Why security?" and I can only answer that I never want to be in the field with someone who thinks a security lecture is unnecessary. We also provide specialized options in the second week, so that students can learn specific research skills or procedures for group-based interpersonal psychotherapy.

Anthony Land MIHA

In 1997, the CIHC introduced a professional course for humanitarian workers that would, for the first time, provide a "license to practice" in crisis situations. Designed as an intensive, four-week course, the IDHA would allow humanitarian practitioners to study history and theory on a postgraduate level. The first iteration of the IDHA took place in Dublin, in July of 1997.

The closing years of the twentieth century, in which the scale and complexity of humanitarian activity expanded rapidly, were the perfect moment for the establishment of an accessible, practical, and academically challenging course for humanitarian professionals. The IDHA has proven a highly successful endeavor: since its inauguration, the course has been taught at least twice every year and has attracted thousands of students. The tireless fundraising of Dr. Cahill and the CIHC, through an extensive network of influential contacts, has enabled us to offer scholarships to students from a substantial number of disaster-affected countries.

Over the course of the IDHA series, there emerged certain topics that generated sufficient interest and material, and that seemed appropriate as standalone, one-week courses. We successfully developed and initiated several of these short courses, one of which includes the MHCE discussed in Lynne's chapter (page 122).

By 2007, flushed with the success of our regular IDHA courses, we realized that our students would benefit from in-depth, one-week modules on a variety of humanitarian topics, and we decided to use this model to build a Master's program. We did, however, recognize that we had to design such a program to meet not only the demanding academic standards of Fordham University, but also the needs of the international community. This resulted in discussions with a broad range of humanitarian organizations in Geneva, held with the objective of fitting the new course as closely as possible to the needs of organizations, which would employ many of our students and graduates.

The program was built by extending the four-week IDHA into a series of four courses. These together formed a Master's Degree that could be taken in segments over a five-year period. The one-week courses that had emerged from the IDHA were incorporated as modules into the MIHA and a series of 11 additional one-week courses were designed and instituted. Two further diplomas, the IDOHA and the IDMA, each require three core modules and one additional module selected from five elective topics. The fourth, the International Diploma in Humanitarian Leadership (IDHL), required completion of two courses and a thesis. The IIHA launched the MIHA in partnership with Fordham University in 2010. The program presented great opportunities for students, but also its own set of problems to be overcome.

Many humanitarian organizations now require senior managers to hold a postgraduate degree, and the MIHA is designed specifically for humanitarian professionals with experience in the field who need to achieve a recognized qualification in order to move up the career ladder. Unlike the residential, one-year courses offered elsewhere, the MIHA allows its students to continue their work in the field and take short periods of time away to study each year.

Structuring the course in this way has simplified matters for our students, but has resulted in some challenges for the faculty, most notably maintaining the motivation of students over a prolonged period. Students who return to demanding jobs immediately after completing one or more short courses often find it difficult to then complete their course papers in a timely manner. Setting the paper topic at the beginning of the course, which allows students to work on the paper in the evenings during the course, has helped, but reminders are frequently required. Writing a thesis towards the end of the MIHA has also proved a tough challenge for some students, but with support and follow-up from faculty, we now see a steady stream of graduations each semester.

Teaching humanitarian affairs today means recognizing that the humanitarian world has entered a period of change and instability. It necessitates presenting courses that can adapt to these changes and remain relevant to the needs of students and the organizations that employ them. The sustainability of the humanitarian system as we know it is under threat, and the cracks are showing in several areas.

One of these cracks is the direct threat to the credibility of the humanitarian funding system. Despite shortfalls of almost 50 percent between the funding appealed for and the funding received, humanitarians do not seem able to demonstrate a corresponding increase in unnecessary suffering and death, which would put pressure on donors to fulfill their obligations. This situation has seriously brought into question the credibility of the system of appeals that are the foundation of international humanitarian funding. It has justified donors' decisions to limit funding—decisions taken in an atmosphere of austerity and populist opposition. However, events unfolding in the conflict areas of the Middle East and the developing famines in Africa seem set to send shock waves through this environment of complacency.

A second area of change is the continued and growing pressure to localize aid, due to the steady emergence of professional aid organizations in areas of humanitarian risk and need. These organizations have gained strength and voice, and are seeking a primacy as independent first responders. In conflict situations, this move is seen as difficult to accomplish, primarily due to concerns regarding the neutrality and impartiality of local organizations. However, in situations of intense complex conflicts, international aid providers have found that supporting local organizations through "remote operations" is the only way to fulfill the humanitarian imperative.

In responding to natural disasters, the movement towards localization is easier. However, it has been the perceived failures of the international response to the Indian Ocean tsunami and the 2010 earthquake in Haiti that have led to the increased role for local organizations in response to less publicized situations, such as Typhoon Haiyan in the Philippines and the earthquake in Nepal. The World Humanitarian Summit addressed this shift to localism with the Grand Bargain, in which the signatories agreed to channel one quarter of humanitarian aid toward local organizations and initiatives.

Although the Global War on Terror may have cooled with the partial withdrawal of troops from Iraq and Afghanistan, the fear of terror, justified by repeated incidents widely spaced around the world, is having a profound effect on the teaching of humanitarian affairs. Even utilizing a strategy of moving the component courses of the MIHA closer to disaster affected areas, visa restrictions, and the cost of travel and tuition, are making completing the course increasingly difficult for students. This is especially the case for students from disaster risk and conflict areas. It is amongst students coming from these areas where the future demand for academic qualification in humanitarian affairs is likely to show the fastest growth, due to the rapid development of aid localization. As I write this article in January 2017, in the midst of IDHA 49 in Kathmandu, it is encouraging to see that half of the class comes from the region or other areas of humanitarian action.

To accommodate the new and future environment, we intend to convert several elements of the MIHA into distance-learning courses, allowing students to complete many parts of the course at home, and to remain employed as they learn. The aim is to minimize the amount of time students need attend residential courses, while maintaining the academic rigor of the course itself. The MIHA is furthering the initial objectives of the IDHA—namely, to provide an accessible, practitioner-based, academically rigorous education in humanitarian action. In doing this, the MIHA is looking to the future and adapting to a changing global environment, in order to produce the right graduates, at the right time, in the right places, to alleviate humanitarian suffering.

Conferences and Publications

As important as the IDHA and our numerous other courses are, university-based conferences and publications provided an equally significant contribution to the emerging discipline of international humanitarian assistance. Shortly after the CIHC's establishment of the IIHA in 2000, we agreed to provide one or more books per year for Fordham University Press (FUP). The International Humanitarian Affairs (IHA) Book Series is intended to provide practical volumes for use by professionals in the field as well as by university students around the world in a wide variety of academic departments. Éditions Robert Laffont has translated the majority of the books into French. Other volumes have been translated into Spanish, German and Arabic. To complement the books of our early years—*Framework for Survival, Directory of Somali Professionals, and Preventive Diplomacy*—the CIHC sponsored a series that ranged from handbooks and technical textbooks to philosophical and historical volumes, all of which are authored or edited by Kevin M. Cahill, M.D.

Basics of International Humanitarian Missions and Emergency Relief Operations (2003)

The IHA Book Series was launched with two practical volumes that were heavily based upon the curriculum that our tutors had developed for the IDHA training courses. In these books we considered the specific challenges dealt with before, during and immediately after disasters. Designed for students, teachers, practitioners, policymakers, journalists, and other professionals, *Basics of Humanitarian Missions and Emergency Relief Operations* covered fundamental concepts, contexts, and problems, in settings that range from floods and earthquakes to medical emergencies, civil strife, and forced migration.

Traditions, Values and Humanitarian Action (2003)

It has always been a core belief of the CIHC community that the richness of humanity lies in its incredible diversity, and that any diminution in that complex mixture diminishes all of us. Imposing uniform standards of behavior, stifling differences of opinion and style, and restricting customs and practices are regressive, usually destructive, acts. *Traditions, Values and Humanitarian Action* tried to answer questions related to the various foundations on which a caring society might be built. Contributors wrote about religions, codes of conduct in varied professions, and the importance of cultural diversity. "Fault lines," those moments where the core foundations of society, due to individual or government actions, begin to crack were examined. UN Secretary-General Kofi Annan provided the Foreword to the book, writing, "First among our shared human values must be the humanitarian instinct, the instinct that drives us to help our fellow human beings in their hour of need, no matter how different from us they may be."

Human Security for All (2004)

In August 2003, our friend and colleague, Sérgio Vieira de Mello, was among those killed in the bombing of the Canal Hotel in Baghdad, Iraq. Only a year earlier, Sérgio had given the Commencement Address at the IDHA, urging fellow humanitarian aid workers to "guide us to the greatest truth, help us transcend the repetitions and contradictions of our earthly experience and—perhaps even more important—to discover the unity of the world."

As a fitting tribute to Sérgio and the other aid workers who lost their lives, the CIHC gathered a number of friends and colleagues at Fordham University to discuss the issue of humanitarian security in a changing world. Sérgio was well aware that in the harsh reality of his work, in the midst of conflict and chaos, there was rarely "neutral space," even for humanitarians. He recognized that "neither dignity nor equality could take root in the absence of basic security."

The 14 years since the attack on the Canal Hotel has seen the death of over 1,500 humanitarian aid workers, as well as increased injuries and kidnappings. As the crises in Syria, South Sudan, Yemen, Iraq, and throughout the world show little sign of abating, this issue will continue to reverberate throughout the humanitarian community for years to come.

Technology for Humanitarian Action (2005)

The growth and influence of technology on all facets of life in the last decades has been incalculable. Humanitarian aid work and response has changed drastically, and continues to evolve, due to the Internet, smartphones, social media, satellite imagery, global mapping, etc. With *Technology for Humanitarian Action*, and the conference that preceded it, the CIHC brought technology experts together with humanitarian aid workers, many for the first time. The book evolved from my work as Chief Medical Advisor on Counterterrorism for the New York Police Department. Scientists associated with the Defense Advanced Research Policy Agency (DARPA) impressed me with their imaginative proposals in devising monitoring techniques to detect and isolate serious biological, chemical and radiation threats to our safety.

As my contact with these men and women deepened I quickly realized how the intellectual and financial resources devoted to defense concerns dwarfed the attention given to the overwhelming, often intractable problems that faced humanitarian workers. This conference and publication were yet another effort by the CIHC to put varied groups, who perhaps had never considered the dilemmas the others faced, together to discuss shared problems and look to future solutions.

To Bear Witness: A Journey of Healing and Solidarity (2005)

As the President of the CIHC, I have often had to serve as the public face and fundraiser of the organization. This collection of some of my editorials, lectures and short essays is the most personal in the IHA Book Series. It encompasses, in my own story, the need that drives one to become a part of humanitarian assistance in the first place. As I wrote in a concluding chapter: "Each individual's tapestry will be blessedly different, and I can only hope that these essays, and the philosophy they express, to you as they do to me, are threads that can be woven into many varied designs." This book was translated into French as *Témoigner* (NiL éditions 2010), and a second, expanded edition was published in 2013.

The Pulse of Humanitarian Assistance (2007)

The wars in Iraq and Afghanistan, and the uncertain role of humanitarians in the years afterward, were the cause for much soul searching and unresolved questions within the international community. Six years after the 9/11 attacks, the CIHC gathered a group or humanitarians to ask not only "Where are we now?" but also "Where are we going?" We used the example of an ancient diagnostic and prognostic tool—monitoring the heartbeat of a sick person—to assess the health of our projects. *The Pulse of Humanitarian Assistance* was the result of our attempts to address issues such as the impact of globalization, military-civilian interaction, the plight of the internally displaced and the reassessment of traditional actions of aid agencies.

As I wrote at the time, "In this sad, almost patently self-destructive era, those of us privileged to work in humanitarian assistance find ourselves struggling to maintain noble traditions when the very foundations of civilization seem to be collapsing. But adhering rigidly to the standard approaches of the past is an almost certain recipe for failure. We should be able to adapt without abandoning fundamental values… We must constantly monitor the pulse, changing our approaches as new problems and new tool develop. As Samuel Beckett once summarized life's journey: 'Try again, fail again, fail better.'"

Even in Chaos: Education in Times of Emergency (2010)

In 2009, my dear friend, Father Miguel D'Escoto Brockmann of Nicaragua, was elected as the President of the Sixty-Third Session of the UN General Assembly. I had known Miguel since the 1960s, sharing in countless joys and setbacks, and was fortunate to serve as his Chief Advisor on Humanitarian Affairs during his tenure at the UN.

Education and the future of youth throughout the world had always been pressing concerns for the CIHC. Miguel asked me to convene, and Chair, a formal thematic debate at the UN Headquarters on the state of education during conflict and post-natural disasters in which experts, in a range of fields, expressed the need to make education a priority in the response to complex emergencies. *Even in Chaos* was the result of that dialogue. As President D'Escoto wrote at the time, "This book advances the international dialogue by identifying steps to protect our schools and ensure that they remain safe and nurturing environments even in the midst of the most difficult conditions."

There was also an Occasional Paper, *Gaza: Destruction and Hope,* published as part of our Book Series during the Presidency of Miguel D'Escoto. I had made an official visit to Gaza after the Israeli invasion in 2009. Before leaving for Gaza I was fortunate to have a briefing from a CIHC Board Director, and IIHA Diplomat in Residence, my dear friend Peter Hansen. His long, distinguished career at the UN concluded with a nine-year assignment as Commissioner-General of the UN Relief and Works Agency for Palestine Refugees in the Near East (UNRWA). In 2010, the UN chose my report on Gaza to distribute worldwide on Humanitarian Day, August 15.

Tropical Medicine: A Clinical Text (2010)

In 2010, after more than 50 years in print, *Tropical Medicine: A Clinical Text* was published as a Jubilee Edition. This eighth edition is available in Spanish and French translations. Medical and public health details are an important consideration in international humanitarian assistance, and this textbook provides the legitimacy and credibility of a professional career that evolved to include the many other dimensions of relief in conflict areas and after natural disasters.

More With Less: Disasters in a Time of Declining Resources (2012)

In 2011, the new PGA, H.E. Nassir Abdulaziz Al-Nasser, asked me to serve as his Chief Advisor on Humanitarian and Public Health Issues. Over the course of that year, in New York and Mogadishu and Doha, I was fortunate to observe Nassir's passion and dedication to his diplomatic work; and privileged to witness his compassion for those in need, his innate decency, and his modesty. President Al-Nasser identified disaster preparedness and response as one of the key objectives that he wished to pursue during his tenure, and it was both my, and the CIHC's, honor to assist with that goal. Al-Nasser's first speech as PGA was at IDHA graduation, and he continues to serve as Diplomat in Residence at the IIHA.

More With Less was an attempt to reflect on a critical issue then facing the UN General Assembly: the reality of diminished resources for relief operations following the global economic meltdown in 2008. In this book, we sought to "find new solutions, rethink strategies, and redefine our actions" to ensure that critically needed donations and efforts were spent in both sustainable and creative ways. The text detailed the CIHC's long-held belief that improvements to humanitarian action happen not despite, but because of, adversity.

Two important books by Ambassador Francis Deng, a Sudanese and later South Sudanese diplomat, and a long-term Director of the CIHC, were also part of our IHA Book Series. Ambassador Deng served as the first UN Special Rapporteur on the Human Rights of Internally Displaced Persons and later as UN Special Advisor for the Prevention of Genocide. These books were intended to provide timely information as the nation of Sudan divided. Sad to say the tragedy predicted in *Sudan at the Brink* has been realized; the second book *Bound by Conflict* provides a glimmer of hope. Francis Deng has sought reconciliation and peace in his homeland for almost a half century. We have worked together since meeting in South Sudan in the early 1960s and I was privileged that he asked me to write the Foreword to both these books.

In 2013, *History and Hope: The International Humanitarian Reader,* a compendium of some of the best chapters from the previous 12 volumes of the IHA Book Series, was published. It was both a personal and professional culmination of the CIHC's work since its inception and it allowed us not only to look back with pride but to also assess the continuity of a struggle that will never be complete. This is the most frequently downloaded text in the over 1,000 FUP titles, and is used in the courses all over the world.

An Unfinished Tapestry (2014) links the challenges of a large domestic public health position with work in complex humanitarian crises after natural disasters or in conflict situations. For six years I directed the health and mental health services in New York State, and was responsible for 80,000 employees and a budget of $8 billion, while simultaneously maintaining contacts in troubled areas of Africa and Central America. Though the problems in the highly developed society of the US were vastly different from those in the war zones of Somalia or Nicaragua, there were amazing similarities in delivering care where resources and expectations were often drastically out of synch with the demands.

Two recent additions to the IHA Book Series, *The Open Door: Art and Foreign Policy at the RCSI* (2014) and *A Dream of Dublin* (2016), provide details on the academic developments of humanitarian affairs in this discipline at the RCSI. The CIHC offered our first IDHA there in 1997, and the College has been a sponsor of every course offered since then. *The Open Door* is a book based on a series of Distinguished Lectures given there with contributions from several Nobel Laureates, artists, political leaders, and CIHC Directors, including Jan Eliasson, who was Sweden's Minister for Foreign Affairs at the time of his talk. Another CIHC Director, Professor Eoin O'Brien, offered a summation at the end of each lecture.

A Dream for Dublin further connects the work of the CIHC, the IDHA, and the IIHA with Ireland. It begins in 1960 with my first lecture at the RCSI, and follows my establishment of a new Department of Tropical Medicine, and its development over 36 years, during which I taught over 4,000 medical students. The book concludes with a chapter on the introduction of humanitarian affairs in this 230-year-old noble and venerable institution, and a gracious reflection by the President of Ireland, Michael D. Higgins.

The Fordham Experience

The relationship between an independent charity such as the CIHC and a university partner could be difficult if there was not mutual respect and the desire to accomplish a common goal. Promoting the essential role of academia was part of our original vision, and we have had joint programs with the United Nations University, the University of Geneva, CUNY, Liverpool University, as well as host universities on all continents. Two academic institutions—the RCSI and Fordham University in New York—have been the primary foundations for our academic efforts.

The CIHC's main charitable activity has been to support our IIHA, first established at Hunter College in 1996. Hunter's President, David Caputo, was an enthusiastic and generous partner, traveling to Switzerland and Ireland to participate in our early graduation ceremonies. However, even he understood our accepting an invitation to move the Institute to Fordham University when its then President, Father Joseph A. O'Hare S.J., offered in 2000 to establish an independent Institute that could involve the many schools of the University, to appoint me as University Professor, and to have the Institute report directly—and solely—to the President in order to avoid the time consuming, and almost inevitable, infighting that a new Institute, with a commitment to provide part of its training in overseas locations, would invite.

Since its inception, Brendan Cahill has been the Executive Director of the IIHA at Fordham, and has skillfully guided the development of a Master's program, an undergraduate Major in Humanitarian Affairs, a combined Bachelor's and Master's, and the very complex financial and logistical problems faced when providing academically acceptable courses all over the world. The Institute boasts a network of alumni from 135 nations, and visa and currency exchange are but a few of the challenges where Brendan's MBA has been indispensable.

He represents the IIHA in our meetings with the Fordham President, Provost, Deans, and Faculty. He negotiated MOUs with IOM, NOHA, and the ICRC. He is, above all, my son of whom I am very proud, and he assists me—in my often confounding medical, clinical, and academic work schedules—with frequent demands for rapid response to a myriad of ideas for the future of the CIHC and IIHA.

Brendan Cahill

The history of the IIHA at Fordham University is an evolution of what came before, and a reflection of the principles that have continued to guide the CIHC since its inception.

My father purposely created the IDHA as a university-accredited program. Institutions that have provided this accreditation include the United Nations University, Liverpool University, the University of Geneva, and—most especially—Fordham University and the RCSI. My father founded the Department of Tropical Medicine at the RCSI, and the Chief Executive of that institution, Michael Horgan, saw great value in the partnership.

In 2001, Father Joseph A. O'Hare S.J., then President of Fordham University, approached my father as the President of CIHC with an offer that would benefit both organizations. He proposed a partnership wherein the CIHC and Fordham would create a separate, complementary Institute, which would report directly to the President of the University. My father was named a University Professor, the highest academic position at Fordham. The independence of the IIHA reporting structure was, and is, critical; only by remaining autonomous from other schools and educational programs could we serve the full Fordham academic community, and the humanitarian one, in a neutral and innovative way. Thanks to independent funding, the Institute has remained free of the budgetary and bureaucratic entanglements that almost always accompany programs within a school or department. Interdisciplinary in nature, and practical in its outcome, the Institute has used the strength of Fordham's faculty to work with the unique contacts of the CIHC Board in the humanitarian sector, thus creating programs that married academic rigor with real-world solutions.

I.   The IDHA and the IIHA

When the IIHA was first founded, the CIHC was operating two IDHA courses per year: one in New York and one in Europe, alternatively in Dublin or Geneva. Larry Hollingworth, the Humanitarian Programs Director, also served as a CIHC representative in certain emergency situations, seconded to UNRWA, UNOCHA, and other agencies in a senior directorial position. The flexibility of his position allowed Larry to remain an active presence in the field, and act as one of the IDHA's most effective ambassadors; his participation in these missions exposed him to other humanitarian workers, who provided him with current case studies, and helped him identify gaps in the internal training of agencies and organizations. Further, he developed his own networks of those who seemed interested in our programs, and whom we might call upon to lecture for future courses. The Board of the CIHC took a comprehensive view of the humanitarian world, but it was Larry who instituted a holistic, familial approach to our educational mission.

I was asked to lead the office for an unspecified time—perhaps six months or so—and concentrate specifically on providing an administrative structure to the IDHA courses. Those six months extended into an immensely satisfying career, over the course of which I have been able to use my own business acumen to expand and sustain the remarkable initiatives that my father established. The IIHA is the only independent Institute on the Fordham campus, and we operate outside of the normal structures of the University. Father O'Hare and his team, especially Dorothy Marinucci, protected us from the professional jealousy and machinations of those who initially didn't understand what we aimed to accomplish or how our success would benefit the entire University. The President provided space for us; offered invitations to collaborate; introduced our staff to vice presidents, deans, faculty members, and administrators who would become our cherished friends and colleagues; and, most of all, encouraged us to do the work of the University.

Fifty courses on, and the IDHA may seem, from the outside, to be a fully self-sufficient endeavor, but this has certainly never been the case. Larry took on a massive amount of work to fill those positions, and we ultimately settled on a staff model that combined the new and the old: we would recruit from a pool of trusted tutors—those who returned year after year—and also offer opportunities to alumni to participate as course lecturers, or as part of the academic staff. In addition, we decided to make better use of the wisdom and experience repre-sented in the Fordham faculty, and soon we had convinced historians, political scientists, economists, anthropologists, sociologists, social work professors, educationists, law professors, business professors, military, and clergy from within the University to offer lectures to our students, or oversee security days. Our collaborative dynamic with the faculty has led to the development of a number of other courses, which are described in more detail later in this chapter.

One of Larry's most enviable skills is his ability to live in the present and offer his undivided attention to any task. He is happy to plan, to reflect on past victories or failures, but I think his true joy is to live the life in front of him. To have an administrator with that skill on our team has been an unexpected boon. Larry can adapt to any circumstance, respond to questions and complications, and reschedule lectures at a moment's notice (fig. page 150). Thanks to his military training, the IDHA team runs like clockwork, even in the midst of daily meetings, debriefs, adjustments.

Once the IIHA established closer relationships within the Fordham faculty, and the University President formally approved the accreditation of the IDHA diploma, I approached the Dean of the Graduate School of Arts and Sciences (GSAS), Dr. Nancy Busch, to discuss academic credit. A well-respected child psychologist, and an administrator with both empathy and imagination, Nancy was an insightful, positive, and strategic leader. She regarded the IDHA as a new style of education, centered upon a universal mission, which could push the GSAS faculty further into the real world. We sat down with the Chairs of the Political Science, Sociology, and Psychology Departments, and built a full curriculum around the IDHA. We adjusted some elements of the diploma, such as cutting the Saturday courses and adding an essay to emphasize critical independent thinking expected in academia. With over 200 hours of tuition—and with a course load that includes weekly exams, presentations, and a research paper—the IDHA indisputably combines academic rigor and praxis, and we feel that the students who complete the course truly earn the eight postgraduate credits.

In partnership with Dr. Busch, we applied for approval from the New York State Department of Education, and received the full credits requested. Dr. Busch then set up an open enrollment period for all who wished to apply for credit, even those who had taken the course earlier, or outside Fordham; she also recognized the value of the IDHA and agreed that any increase in the tuition would place unreasonable limits on our international student body. Unlike business school students in the United States, who can avail themselves of grants, scholarships, and loans, our students are predominately international and must rely on ever-smaller training grants from their employers, or support from the CIHC. When students ask why the IDHA seems so expensive, I tell them that the eight credits alone should cost $14,000.

Because we include a full month's room and board, as well as academic material, class trips, social events, and graduation gifts, the real value of the IDHA comes to almost $20,000 in 2017.

In 2003, only three years after the IIHA opened its doors, the Reverend Joseph M. McShane S.J., succeeded Father O'Hare as the President of Fordham University. We knew a new University President might not prioritize our humanitarian initiative as his predecessor had, but our fears proved entirely unfounded: in the 14 years since he assumed the Presidency, Father McShane has championed the work of the Institute, participated in our courses, distributed copies of our books to incoming freshmen as a welcome gift, and in every respect, acted as our strongest supporter and ally within the University. His introduction on the first day of our IIHA classes is something of a legend among our students, as is his knowledge of Catholic and Jesuit schools in Pakistan, Zimbabwe, Ecuador, and many other countries around the world.

I also thank the Provost of the University, Dr. Stephen Freedman, and his Chief of Staff, Ellen Fahey Smith. Both have ensured that we are involved in the University's academic planning process, and that we continue to receive the personal support of Dr. Freedman and Father McShane for any new projects.

II.   The Short Courses and the MIHA

The CIHC developed its second course, a one-week program in Humanitarian Negotiation, in 2002; a third course, based in the Global South, soon followed. We continued to fill in the gaps in humanitarian education, and to create new courses to address the needs identified by our alumni and lecturers. In the process, we expanded our contacts within the University, particularly within GSAS and Fordham School of Law. We partnered with the Leitner Center for Law and Justice for a course on human rights training, and with the Graduate School of Social Service for a course on community participation and mobilization.

With so many programs in the works, I approached Dr. Busch once more to propose the establishment of a postgraduate degree that would later evolve into the MIHA. Tony Land, who was finishing his doctorate at the time, was instrumental in crafting the curricula and bibliography that accompanied the proposal. I met with each department and Graduate Chair, and all relevant faculty in GSAS, in order to receive input and feedback. For the most part, those whom I approached seemed enthusiastic about the idea; only a few voiced concerns about the effect our Master's program might have on their own programs, but we were able to allay their fears.

The New York State Department of Education approved our application, and we launched the first MIHA. My father secured a substantial transfer grant from his Tropical Disease Center at Lenox Hill Hospital, with the support of its Chief Executive, Michael Dowling. This grant provides critical scholarships and administrative funding that continues to support us.

The MIHA promotes a radical style of education, one that is unique to Fordham and, indeed, has few peers anywhere in the world. The program is designed for mid-career humanitarian professionals; our students are typically in their early or mid-thirties—the average age is 38 years old—and have already spent time in the field. Most are employed at international organizations and cannot take off a full year to complete a Master's Degree. Because of the sudden nature of humanitarian work, which requires our students to be deployed in a matter of hours or days, the MIHA does not follow a 12-week semester. Instead, the courses are short, residential, and intensive, like the IDHA, and 90 percent are held in international locations. The IIHA also provides an exclusive link to Fordham, and our academic team is drawn from both University faculty, who join our courses on their own time, and an ever-changing team of outside experts. Fordham faculty members thereby have the opportunity to interact with fellow lecturers and students from all over the world, and to discuss the real-world applications of their own research.

In 2016, the CIHC received generous funding from the Womadix Fund to underwrite distance-learning programs based on our courses. These funds will soon allow a new audience to take these courses, and help create an ever-more interconnected world of humanitarian workers.

III.   NOHA

In the early years of the Institute, one of our dear friends, Dirk Salomons, served as the Director of the prestigious School of International and

Public Affairs at Columbia University. Each June, he would recruit a contingent of students from NOHA, a consortium of European universities that offer a joint degree in Humanitarian Studies. One of the consortium's founders, Dr. Julia Gonzalez, asked the IIHA to take a more active role in the program, since our programs at Fordham closely complemented the NOHA curriculum.

When Dirk retired, NOHA overhauled its Master's program, and requested that Fordham and the IIHA replace Columbia as their US partner. Our relationship with NOHA has been a long and fruitful one: not only do we supervise their third semester students, but as of 2017, we have also co-hosted international conferences, both in Europe and the United States; partnered on a peer review for the Journal of International Humanitarian Action; and will soon establish our student exchange program at the Master's level.

IV.   The Helen Hamlyn Senior Fellow and Internal Staff

Helen Hamlyn joined the CIHC Board in 2002, and established an annual grant that has allowed us to hire an academic fellow and expand our undergraduate programs. We selected Carlos Mejia—an IDHA alumnus and Colombian humanitarian aid worker, who was a child refugee himself —as our first Helen Hamlyn Senior Fellow. Carlos helped us reach out to the other members of the Association of Jesuit Colleges and Universities, and develop new methods to solidify our network of students and faculty.

Dr. Arancha Garcia, a Spanish sociologist, joined us as a Senior Fellow after Carlos, and taught undergraduate courses and conducted research on our behalf throughout the world. She was then succeeded by Dr. Alexander van Tulleken, another IDHA alumnus. Alex used his medical skills and practical experience in Sudan, as well as his charismatic teaching ability, to develop classes on both the graduate and—crucially—the undergraduate level. The IIHA is deeply indebted to, and thankful for, all of our Hamlyn Fellows for their contributions.

We have also been blessed with an excellent administrative team from the start. Our courses are extremely complex to create, oversee, and promote, and the role of the administrator is often overlooked unless a problem arises, in which case they are then vilified. Ellen Bratina,

Alexandra DeBlock, Laura Risimini, and Chrissie Cahill have all done remarkable work on the programmatic and finance side, while Jenna Felz supported both the publications and undergraduate programs. Kasia Laskowski, who joined our team as an unpaid intern, traveled the world with Larry as the Course Administrator, and later worked as our Program Officer in New York, where she created the IIHA newsletter, alumni networks, and social media platforms. Suzanne Arnold also held together many courses as a Course Administrator. I celebrate all of our staff and I name them individually, because the IIHA would not have succeeded without their efforts.

In the years prior to the creation of our undergraduate curricula, more and more Fordham students started to approach me, or another member of the Institute, to sponsor and guide their independent studies of humanitarian affairs. Eventually, I asked the Dean of Fordham's Lincoln Center campus, Reverend Robert Grimes, S.J., if he would support a Minor in Humanitarian Studies. Together, we created a curriculum, brought it before faculty for critiques, and—satisfied that we had built a highly interdisciplinary model—started to offer formal courses.

The Minor was a resounding success, and Father Grimes proposed that the IIHA expand the program into a full undergraduate major. Following our model of collaboration, cooperation, and consideration, we quickly developed the Major—thanks in large part to Dr. van Tulleken —and it has since become one of the fastest growing at Fordham.

The Institute has been fortunate, too, in terms of the Fordham admin-istration: with the enthusiastic backing of the University President and the Provost—and with the support of the current head of GSAS, Dean Eva Badowska, and the Associate Dean, Dr. Melissa Labonte—we contin-ue to explore new ways to advance Humanitarian Studies as a strategic priority within the Fordham curriculum. Father McShane has often called the IIHA "the jewel in the crown of Fordham," as our mission and our global outreach personify the highest goals of the University.

Throughout the IIHA's history, we have worked hard to create opportunities for younger people, creating internships both within the Institute and with partner organizations in the UN and the NGO community in New York. These internships often lead to employment within the humanitarian sector.

V.   Master of Science in Humanitarian Studies

The average undergraduate Humanitarian Studies student has a second major, is motivated by social justice issues, and aims to enter the humanitarian sector. We therefore wanted to create a new Master's program that would furnish our undergraduate students with the skills needed to work in the nonprofit world.

We worked closely with Dr. Labonte to devise a curriculum based on practical skills that our students would find useful today, such as accounting and data analysis. The curricula also featured a strong interdisciplinary component, with courses and subjects drawn from history, philosophy, and political science. Perhaps most importantly, the program allows our students to make full use of IIHA resources and contacts, and to cultivate relationships with NOHA, the Jesuit University Humanitarian Action Network (JUHAN), our alumni network, our formal and informal partners, and our friends in the field.

VI.   Publications

In addition to academic courses, the IIHA has produced many publications, most of which are available from FUP under our IHA Book Series. My father is a prolific and fluid writer, and a persuasive and driven editor. Thanks to the foresight of the FUP Directors, particularly Fred Nachbaur, our publications are perhaps the greatest legacy of the Institute. Of the thousands of titles available in FUP's century-old catalogue, ours are the most downloaded. Used all over the world in graduate and undergraduate programs, and by policy and political experts, our publications form the bedrock of all of our educational programs.

VII.   Move to Rose Hill

In 2017, the IIHA moved to Fordham's Rose Hill campus in the Bronx. The decision was not made lightly, but after 16 years at the Lincoln Center campus in Manhattan, it became apparent that we had outgrown the space, and that we could not adequately meet the needs of the undergraduate population at Rose Hill, nor expand and develop our research areas. The new location will also allow for classes, lectures, and exhibitions, none of which we could offer at the Lincoln Center offices.

VIII.   Conferences and Research

The Institute has been fortunate to host numerous international conferences at Fordham, which led to the publication of books on themes as disparate as *Traditions and Values in Humanitarian Action, to Technology in the Humanitarian Action,* to *Education in Times of Emergencies.* We have hosted countless lunchtime lecturers, screened films, and provided a venue for debates.

Our move to Rose Hill will allow us to deepen our research areas; the Humanitarian Innovation Hub is one of our newest, and most exciting, initiatives. Led by Innovation Fellow Giulio Coppi, the Hub will look at block chain and data analysis, and work with partners in academia, the private sector, and in the humanitarian sphere, in order to contribute to the future of humanitarian response.

IX.   Last Thoughts

The book in your hands holds stories of relationships, friendships, and moments in the classroom that changed the lives of our students. These stories are all true; our courses create a space for these decidedly personal, non-academic revelations, and that is mostly the result of the semi-permanent team of individuals who run our programs, and share the same philosophy of love and humanity.

This philosophy can be traced back to the founding of the CIHC, which started with the strong feeling that humanitarian responders needed a "license to operate." Without the combination of passion and compassion, would-be humanitarian professionals end up in any number of fields. Each year, in each course, participants from vastly different walks of life come together, if only for a week or a month. We treat all of our students as equals; we believe that their opinions are worth exploring, that their experiences add nuance to the lessons learned. Some, when they arrive, don't understand this approach, and they are guarded, or proud, or reticent.

The IDHA is a family. Our courses are unique because of our culture of passion and compassion, and because of the generosity of all who are involved. From Pamela Lupton Bowers, who flies, often at her own expense, so that our newest group of strangers can be molded into teams; to Kofi Annan, who made sure to videotape an introduction to our course for his entire term at the UN; to Boutros Boutros-Ghali, who once hosted the IDHA 17 students on a Nile boat ride with whirling dervishes. Our relationships, our friendships, flow from the classroom to the dining room to late night conversations. As a student, and now as part of the staff, I cannot tell you when the most education comes, but I can say that a culture of love and absolute generosity imbues every program we have ever run.

Fordham University has played a great role in the history of our programs. Its leaders have allowed the faculty the opportunity to move their research into this sphere and, most importantly, have recognized that some contributions can only come from outside experts. Fordham has provided our innovative Institute with a home and a community in which we can grow and influence the world on the University's behalf.

None of our work could have been accomplished without external funding, and while I have focused on expanding our programs and running the IIHA, my father has devoted much of his boundless energy and skills to securing gifts and grants to support scholarships, visiting lecturers, and creating a space for the free exchange of ideas on how to make humanitarian aid more effective. He has corralled senior diplomatic, artistic, and humanitarian figures to lecture to our small classes, write chapters for our books, and participate in our conferences.

Scholarships has been given to those local and national staff who would never otherwise have the means to attend our courses. My father had a vision to change humanitarian education, and he has spent the better part of his life raising the funds and linking his disparate professional interests—medical, literary, diplomatic—to achieve that vision. Whatever the IIHA has achieved, all of it is due to the founding vision and careful direction of my father. The credit belongs to him alone. The Institute is the natural result of his ingenuity and leadership, and a true testament to his imagination and energy.

For nearly two decades, at every graduation, I approach the end of the ceremony with mixed emotions. I look out at the class and know it is likely the last time I will see all of us together, in one room. Some of our students I may never see again. We will keep in touch, of course, through emails or video chats or Facebook, but the magic of the past few weeks cannot be recaptured.

Yet I find comfort in the fact that our students will soon be out in the world, aiding the vulnerable, bearing witness to injustice, advocating against the obscenity of poverty, and contributing to their communities, each in their own special way. They are neither saints nor sinners; they are exactly like me, and yet completely different from me, praying to their God as I pray to mine, holding their loved ones as I hold mine, mourning their losses—private and professional—as I do mine. As I look out on those familiar faces, I celebrate our similarities and our differences, our shared humanity and our individual dreams for the future. I know that our time together has produced something new, something wonderful, something that neither time, nor distance, nor even death itself, can erase; and I am proud to have played my part.

Brendan Cahill (left), Executive Director of the IIHA,
and Larry Hollingworth (right),
Humanitarian Programs Director of the CIHC

Donors

The tuition fee for the IDHA is $5,500—covering room and board for a full month, 200-plus hours program. It is one of the great educational bargains of our time. To permit candidates from the developing world to participate, a scholarship fund was an essential prerequisite for this component of our dream to materialize. Fortunately, the CIHC has secured adequate funds to allow full or partial scholarships for over 1,500 candidates from over 135 nations to attend both the IDHA and the ancillary courses that represent every discipline needed in a successful response to a complex humanitarian crisis.

Much of the financial support has come from individual donors, though we have certainly been grateful for institutional grants. Since the CIHC is a public charity, all donors can be identified in our tax filings. Most are friends and patients who sought no acknowledgement beyond the personal satisfaction of contributing to an important effort to improve the world, alleviate suffering, and promote mutual understanding and peace.

Critical financial support came shortly after our founding in 1992. A Scottish publisher, Mr. George Craig, sold his Family Christian Book Stores, and donated $250,000 for conferences and new educational endeavors; this was a critical "seed" grant.

Every year, Herbert Allen, as I note in the dedication of *History and Hope,* has provided "steady, generous support for academic initiatives that have changed dreams into realities." John Hess not only provided the invaluable services of Al Marchetti, the Hess Corporation's Chief Financial Officer, to advise on our fiscal and tax policies, but also gave a grant defraying the global communication costs of the CIHC. On several occasions, the CIHC Secretary, Lord David Owen complemented his own donation by securing corporate grants from companies on whose Boards he served.

After Paul Hamlyn's death, his widow, Helen, joined our Board, bringing her vitality and desire to effect change in the fields of design, education and welfare, and healthy ageing. In 2004, she endowed the Helen Hamlyn Fellowship within the IIHA at Fordham University.

Mrs. Betty Wold Johnson and the Johnson Foundation have been annual donors for the full 25 years of the CIHC's existence. Another Director of the CIHC, Geraldine Kunstadter, has provided several scholarships per year for many years. Johanna Hill and her Womadix Fund provided a major grant to promote the development of distance learning techniques for selected humanitarian courses. When my personal secretary of 41 years, Joan Durcan, died, a scholarship fund to help IDHA candidates was established under her name. Claudia and Albert Ziegler have given 5 full scholarships to this fund; the total for the Durcan Fund is now well over $150,000, and growing. My sons, and our family KMC Foundation, have been most supportive of CIHC projects.

It is impossible to express here my personal gratitude to the hundreds of donors to the CIHC and IIHA. Many gave non-fiscal gifts that were essential. To establish a proper legal entity that allowed us not only to define our goals but to permit deductible donations that would be required to fund our dreams, Cyrus Vance had his law firm, Simpson Thatcher, draw up the necessary legal papers for establishing a new public charity corporation in New York State. All this time consuming work, and subsequent filings with tax agencies, were done as a pro bono gift. Martin Deutsch and the US Travel Association arranged for gratis or discounted airfares for our teachers; Aer Lingus also provided major travel support for tutors; the late Massimo Vignelli kindly designed many of our books, and this has been continued by his protégé, Mauro Sarri; Leo McGinity, Jr. has offered pro bono legal advice since the founding of the CIHC.

To select for this book one donor's rationale as an example of why people give, I present the reflections of Orsa Lumbroso. She originally gave a single IDHA scholarship through her family's Besso Foundation in gratitude for medical care for her husband, Luca. As of this date, she has provided 82 full scholarships, and Besso Scholars are now working in crisis areas for the UN and NGOs all over the world.

Orsa Lumbroso

My very dear and infinitely estimable Dr. Kevin Cahill,

Thank you for asking me to contribute to this book. Your request has moved me: it is an honor, and I will not attempt to disguise my delight at being in a position to express the boundless admiration I feel for your decision to live not so much for yourself, as for your "hungering neighbor."

From our first phone call in 2000, it was clear to me that I was very lucky to be speaking to you. I was reminded at once of my great-grandfather, Marco Besso, and of the Foundation in Rome that bears his name, which he established over a century ago with goals that in essence are not very different from yours.

You, like Marco Besso, have placed at the very center of your being a passion for an informed and empathic awareness of the individual person, for life, and whatever this basic thinking may lead to: Marco in finance, and you in medicine. These may seem to be efforts that are worlds apart, if they are not indeed judged—with a certain superficiality—to be irreconcilable. But this is a mistake, and not just because of what you have done and continue to do every day for a better and more just world, and not only because for so many years, the Foundation that Marco started has been helping to support IDHA with annual study grants!

Soon after you helped my husband Luca, we developed a great esteem for one another, even though we didn't know each other in person. One day, you told me you were going to Switzerland to attend the IDHA training course you had conceived and organized. I wanted to understand better, and asked you to explain the purpose and the topic; and for me that was an important moment. I saw a connection between your words and the ideals that moved my grandfather to create the Fondazione Marco Besso and Ernesta Besso in 1918.

It was clear for me that I would present to the Board of Marco Besso this IDHA initiative to give support in critical situations caused by natural disasters or conflicts. I asked for more practical information to better organize the scholarships that, by statute, must be given to Italian citizens.

The Board in 2001 unanimously approved the project, which from an ethical point of view was so akin to the Fondazione's original intent. Between two to five scholarships would be given each year for the New York and Geneva IDHA training courses, depending on availability. I nominate successful candidates, assisted by the Vice President of the Fondazione, Cipriana Scelba, who had already devoted herself in the aftermath of the liberation of Rome to the care and organization of cultural exchanges with the United States, and who served from 1948 to 1988 as the Director of the Fulbright program in Italy. At this point, I have to say I learned with great interest that many Italians give their support in various crisis situations around the world and were very interested to attend the IDHA. Cipriana Scelba always asks to receive a letter from the Besso Fellows at the end of their course work. These letters are a precious reminder of just how appreciated the lessons and meetings with other participants have been. I always feel a strong sense of gratitude toward Dr. Cahill and the CIHC.

It was not hard for me–even at that first meeting of the Board of the *Fondazione*, after my friendship with Dr. Cahill had become a sharing of work and hope for a world that would be less aggressively self-seeking and more genuinely inclined towards mutual recognition; even as the dispossessed throughout the world faced increasingly bitter sufferings–to understand why the Fondazione, of which my mother was then the President, should support Dr. Cahill's efforts with study grants.

Marco Besso's home is the location of his Fondazione today: he created it for increasing dialogue among those who hope for a world not of antagonism, but of joy in human solidarity, because we are all of us human.

Thank you, Kevin, for giving me this chance to express the shared ideals of a shared history, for everyone has the right to a life of peace, and not of hatred and competitive acts of aggression.

With affection and boundless respect from your friend,

Orsa Lumbroso
Rome, Italy

Preventive Diplomacy

This final chapter circles back to the ideas and activities of the early years of the CIHC. At a recent talk at the United Nations Headquarters, reiterating our focus on the importance of promoting the centrality of humanitarian affairs in international diplomatic dialogue, I noted:

Boutros Boutros-Ghali played many roles in a long and full life; some can be captured in the various titles that characterized his decades of public service. There were common threads that linked these official roles into a cohesive tapestry, but only those privileged to know Boutros on a personal level could fully appreciate the exceptional qualities that made him such a unique individual. I knew him for many decades as his physician, confidant and friend. He was a fiercely independent man, one of exceptional integrity and honesty, with an endearing, self-effacing humor. He possessed a rare modesty and humility that came from a long noble struggle to help his nation, family, friends, and a world in desperate need of his generous insights.

The topic I have chosen for this UN Lecture in honor of Secretary General Boutros Boutros-Ghali is one that was very close to his heart. In a final interview, shortly before his death on February 16, 2016, at age 93, reflecting on his life's work, Boutros was asked what he considered his most important legacy: he responded, "My work with Doctor Cahill in the mid-1990s on preventive diplomacy." There is a lovely story behind that response. For many years, Leia, Boutros, my wife Kate, and I would gather for a weeklong retreat to discuss difficult issues that were likely to arise in the UN or other international debates. From these retreats came many long-term projects, including his commitment to preventive diplomacy.

Boutros, in a remarkable gesture of confidence in the importance of creative ideas, and in the capacity of his physician to explore—and explain—the concepts of a new and comprehensive approach to preventive diplomacy, asked, in 1995, that I convene and chair a plenary conference on the concept at the UN. The invited speakers were to view the topic through the prism of public health, seeing if the latter's strict methodology could bring clarity to the vague outlines and approaches that characterize diplomacy. Speakers were asked to present their arguments using the universally understood semantics of health, disease, and medicine.

Ambassadors, as well as the general public, often use common medical words, and diplomats can readily adapt these terms in explaining the evils of spreading discord, and the multiple methods employed in efforts to restore peace. Conflicts—like malignant tumors—can metastasize if appropriate therapy is not provided, can become endemic in innocent populations, defying early diagnoses. There are contagious effects in conflicts that may cause political paralysis, and the hemorrhaging of societal understanding leading to mental scars, post traumatic psychological syndromes, physical deformities, amputations, the terminology of sexual assaults and the escalation to epidemic levels of uncontrolled local feverish fighting. We talk of the search, usually futile, for instant cures, for DNA-like analyses of impending strife, of seeking the proper peacekeeping prescriptions for warring patients, of using quarantine and isolation to contain diseased states with diplomatic tools, of maintaining treatment protocols until remission is realized by adjusting the dosages of, for example, sanctions.

So also, with Preventive Diplomacy, we suggested that it might be helpful to use public health cost-benefit examples to justify the large expenditures often necessary to alleviate conflict-prone situations. In conflict resolutions one tries to identify obstacles to—and blockages in—the search for peace as if one were diagnosing and treating an impaired circulatory system. We can argue for the long-term involvement of peacekeeping operations by citing preventive chemotherapy, and the public understands such analogies. These are but a few of the benefits of utilizing universally known medical terms to explain the often arcane goals and methods of diplomacy, goals that must now convince a citizenry that demands increasing transparency to sustain costly international interventions and relief operations.

The conference speakers included leading figures at the UN including Boutros as Secretary-General; Kofi Annan, then in charge of peace-keeping operations; Peter Hansen, Commissioner-General of UNRWA; Jan Eliasson, the first Undersecretary-General of the UN Department of Humanitarian Affairs (UNDHA); the former US Secretary of State; the former Foreign Ministers of the United Kingdom, France, Sweden, and Sudan; the President of the International Court of Justice in The Hague; the Secretary-General of the Organization of African Unity, as well as distinguished Professors and a Nobel Peace Prize Laureate. I edited the manuscripts into book form, and that text, in follow-up editions and translations, is widely used in academic and diplomatic training programs throughout the world.

One of the supreme creations of the human spirit is the idea of prevention. Like liberty and equality, it is a seminal concept drawn from a reservoir of optimism that centuries of epidemics, famines and wars have failed to deplete. It is an amalgam of hope and possibility, which assumes that misery is not an indefinable mandate of fate, a punishment only redeemable in a later life, but a condition that can be treated like a disease, and, sometimes, cured, or even prevented.

During a lifetime in the practice of medicine—in Africa, the Middle East, Asia, and Latin America, as well as my own country—I have seen the daily wonders of the healing arts: lives rescued from once-fatal cancers, disease outbreaks miraculously cut short by new drugs and vaccines, and countless millions of people saved from communicable diseases such as polio and smallpox. Indeed, the conquest of smallpox, one of history's deadliest scourges, is itself a triumph of prevention attributable not only to Edward Jenner's inoculation, but to the skills and untiring efforts of thousands of public health workers over a span of 200 years.

I also follow, on a daily basis in the practice of medicine, the wisdom of Hippocrates' adage from 2,500 years ago, "primum non nocere"—first, do no harm—and to try to help those who seek my care without indulging in public comments to anyone but the patient, family and professional colleagues collaborating in difficult clinical situations.

Caught up in hawkish rhetoric, diplomats and politicians too often embark on interventions without carefully considering the consequences. In today's world of instant communications, and the apparent need for politicians to appear to personally solve every problem, the fundamental principles of medical practice—careful reasoning, civil dialogue, and a balanced consideration of different options in devising an optimal course of therapy—are frequently absent in political/diplomatic decision-making.

In working with Boutros to refine an approach to preventive diplomacy it was only natural for me to think of clinical and public health models in contemplating the disorders threatening the health of the world community as it emerged from the rigid alignments of the Cold War and groped for new organizing principles in an age of high technology, global economic competition and multipolar politics. For power balances, realpolitik, and the other blunt-edged tools of East-West confrontation simply did not fit the need for far more subtle, creative, and prospective approaches to the problems complicating the search for peace.

Wanton killing and brutality within supposedly sovereign borders, ethnic and religious strife, millions of starving or near-starving refugees, other millions of migrants fleeing their homes out of fear for their lives or in a desperate search for a better life, human rights trampled down, appalling poverty in the shadows of extraordinary wealth, inhumanity on an incredible scale in what was supposed to be a peaceful dawn following the end of the Cold War: these were the awesome challenges that faced us, and they were quite different from the nation-state rivalries and alliances that preoccupied statesmen during most of the twentieth century.

There had to be a new mindset where diplomats would try to sense dangers before crises exploded, invest in early warning exercises, and intervene, if necessary, at latent stages of conflicts. Some problems—maybe most—have no immediate solutions, but the good public health professional, using all the data of epidemiology and public persuasion, can be positioned to intercede effectively whenever necessary. Diplomats must learn to deal with causes before they are results, to probe societal and political problems when the stress is still manageable, to honor crisis avoidance even more than crisis management.

But if preventive diplomacy is to replace traditional reactive diplomacy, there must be fundamental changes in our international approaches. At present, only problems that attain crisis proportions seem to attract the attention of politicians or diplomats. Our leaders simply are not attuned to deal with incipient disorders at a time when prevention is possible. This will not change easily, especially because journalists, even more in an age of instant information overload, will always prefer to report dramatic conflicts and so-called resolutions rather than the non-story, in their minds, of an avoided tragedy.

Preventive diplomacy emphasizes earlier diagnoses and new kinds of therapy. Underlying causes have to be attacked sooner rather than later, before they become fulminating infections that rage beyond rational control or political containment. This is the defining principle of this new preventive diplomacy, which argues that social detection and early intervention should be as honored in international relations as political negotiation and military response. In its pristine form, the idea is simplicity itself; it is reason opposed to irrationality, peace preferred to violence. In the reality of a disordered world, however, preventive diplomacy is incredibly more complex and, in some respects, controversial.

People can disagree on how to define social health and political disease. The tensions between rights and obligations may seem to be intractable. Force sometimes can be necessary to achieve social progress, so it cannot always be condemned. But while violence may be understandable, it rarely leads towards lasting peace. The very breadth of this view of preventive diplomacy suggests that the term itself is far more restrictive than its purpose and conception. For diplomacy, as it has been practiced during most of a now-dying Industrial Age, had been centered on the idea of nation states dealing with each other on a government to government basis with the help of professionals specializing in secret negotiations and political conspiracy.

Today, however, international relations have been utterly transformed by instant communication, by better informed and more active publics, by the spread of market capitalism, the fragmentation of politics and a veritable explosion of commercial transactions and non-governmental activism. Even the supposedly bedrock principle of national sovereignty has been eroded. Furthermore, preventive diplomacy indicates the many disparate efforts aimed at the maintenance of international peace and security is not a matter for diplomats alone. For the current sources of human stress, community breakdown, and group violence are far too diverse and too deeply embedded in social change to be consigned to the windowless compartments of conventional diplomacy. Many problems do not move in a straight line but rather in endless gyres of cause and effect, so that a fall in coffee prices, for example, can trigger economic unrest, genocide, and precipitate fleeing refugees, starvation, cholera, dysentery and other diseases that overwhelm medical workers and relief organizations.

The patterns Boutros and I discussed in the 1990s concerning Rwanda and the Balkans have re-emerged decades later in Syria and Afghanistan, Iraq and the Occupied Territories of Palestine. The cycles of disaster and the search for solutions involve many different disciplines, including medicine, so that prevention calls for a symphony rather than a solo performance by a single profession like diplomacy. It also calls for a new kind of diplomat. But diplomats, unlike physicians, have not fully accepted a preventive ethos and a disciplined method of using tools to avoid conflicts. If that thesis is valid, then the orchestra clearly needed a knowledgeable and committed conductor capable of promoting preventive diplomacy around the world. Secretary-General Boutros Boutros-Ghali assumed that mantle at the UN.

I had long suggested to Boutros that health and humanitarian issues should be the pragmatic as well as the symbolic centerpiece of the UN. If the Organization was founded to beat weapons into ploughshares, then the fiscal and political focus on military peacekeeping was misplaced. The basic question we discussed, over and over, was how to best present the arguments for an emphasis on preventive diplomacy. I suggested to him that the methodology of public health, and even the universally understood semantics and metaphors of medicine, provided a unique basis for a new type of diplomacy.

Five hundred years ago, Machiavelli, utilizing an apt medical analogy, noted, "When trouble is sensed well in advance, it can easily be remedied; if you wait for it to show, any medicine will be too late because the disease will have become incurable. As the doctors say of a wasting disease, to start with it is easy to cure but difficult to diagnose; after a time, unless it has been diagnosed and treated at the outset, it becomes easy to diagnose but difficult to cure. So it is in politics."

There are several important lessons in that quote. The shrewd and cynical Machiavelli knew that health images would help make his message clear to a skeptical public, and he unapologetically linked medicine and politics as part of life.

162

The origins of violence, especially obvious in today's world, clearly lie in incubating prejudices and injustices that inevitably breed contention. But how rarely are these evil forces exposed early enough, or fought with effective tools before predictable disaster strikes. In preventive medicine one begins by searching for fundamental causes, for the etiology of a disease, and for techniques that can interrupt transmission before serious signs and symptoms become obvious and irreversible damage occurs. If a fatal disease threatens to spread, health experts devise control programs based on careful research and laboratory experiments, sophisticated statistical studies and models, field trials and double-blind surveys that try to minimize biases and biological variants, which often contaminate the best intentioned projects. When deaths do occur, scrupulous postmortem analyses are customary, so that the errors of the past become the building blocks for a better approach to the future. One should, we both believed, be able to adapt this approach to the epidemiology of conflict.

Diplomatic exercises should be subjected to similar probes and autopsies. Nations, particularly great powers and international organizations, must become humble enough to learn from failed efforts rather than merely defending traditional practices. If there are new actors in world conflicts, and a new global environment created by, among other factors, a communication revolution, then the therapeutics of international mediation must change. Unfortunately, public figures are obsessed with dramatic solutions, with a fire brigade approach that assures a continuation of catastrophes.

The international system is always in transition and the contours of the post-Cold War age are still far from clear. But there are already a number of fascinating trends that are central to the development of the preventive diplomacy concept. One is a tentative shift in the direction of individualism that focuses international attention on personal human rights rather than only on the rights and privileges of national sovereignty. Medicine and public health also teach us that diplomatic tools are more effective than coercion. In the case of AIDS, for example, attempts to curb the disease through legal enforcement failed. Only persuasion, education, and cooperation had any success in altering lifestyles that contributed to the problem. In the same way, force has proven to be a poor treatment for violence. Indeed, military intervention and sanctions often do more harm than good. And that is the attraction of preventive diplomacy in international relations—to stop wars before they start.

Even if, as we must fully expect, that noble goal proves elusive, this approach offers the best, and maybe the only viable alternative to the failed practices of the past. Even after conflicts have begun, this new diplomacy, based on a philosophy that focuses on root causes and promotes early involvement can help de-escalate violence and hasten the restoration of peace. The development of sanitation, vaccines, and, more recently, environmental controls have produced phenomenal progress against the enemies of health. In the case of human societies, the promotion of liberal democracy and individual rights marked an historic advance beyond such ancient concepts as slavery and the divine right of kings.

It was for these many reasons we believed that 50 years after the founding of the UN, there was the possibility that the principle of prevention just might take its place as a significant improvement over inaction or coercion in dealing with conflict, and we were determined to try. We knew there were no final answers to offer; there cannot be in our finite and imperfect state. But in the presence of disease, there is common pain that makes no distinctions of race or religion or class or wealth. No matter where medical disaster strikes, all the strands of shared humanity converge in shared suffering. A tumor or a tubercular lesion or an arrhythmia present in an identical manner, and it makes no difference whether the patient is an ambassador or a street cleaner.

I shall now provide, in some detail, ideas that Boutros delivered in a powerful keynote address to the 1995 UN Conference, where he used, as you will appreciate, many similes and analogies of medical parlance. Most of what I shall present here are direct quotes from his speech. Almost in the role of a public health professional, he opened his talk by noting that in matters of peace and security, as in medicine, prevention is self-evidently better than cure. It saves lives and money and it forestalls suffering.

Boutros began by noting:

The main types of such preventive action available at the UN are the use of diplomatic techniques to prevent disputes arising, prevent them from escalating into armed conflict if they do arise, and if that fails, to prevent the armed conflict from spreading. The Secretary-General can use negotiation, inquiry, mediation, conciliation, arbitration, and judicial settlement; resort to regional agencies or arrangements; or try any other peaceful means, which the protagonists may choose. To these techniques can be added confidence-building measures, a therapy that can produce good results if the patients—that is, the hostile parties— will accept it. Central of course to the idea of preventive diplomacy is the assumption that the protagonists are not making effective use of techniques on their own initiative and that the help of a third party is needed.

The techniques employed in preventive diplomacy are the same as those employed in peacemaking—which, in UN parlance, is a diplomatic activity, and not the restoration of peace by forceful means. The only real difference between preventive diplomacy and peacemaking is that the one is applied before armed conflict has broken out and the other thereafter. But today, as in health, there are many endemic situations where the causes of conflict are deeply rooted and chronic tension is punctuated from time to time by acute outbreaks of virulent fighting. In such cases it may be artificial to make a distinction between preventive diplomacy and peacemaking or indeed between preventive and post conflict peace building. Those who want to help control and cure such chronic maladies need to maintain their efforts over a long period of time, varying the therapies they prescribe as the patient's condition improves or deteriorates.

One is sometimes asked to give examples of successful preventive diplomacy. It is not always easy to do so. Confidentiality is usually essential in such endeavors, as it is in the practice of medicine. Time may have to pass before one can say with assurance that success has been achieved. Many different peacemakers may have been at work, and it can sound presumptuous for just one of them to claim the credit.

Preventive humanitarian action addresses, in addition to its healing purpose of bringing relief to those who suffer, the political goal of correcting situations, which, if left unattended, could increase the risk of conflict. A wide range of measures can be required. They can include planning for the humanitarian action that will be required if a crisis occurs, such as stockpiling relief goods in certain places; or they can include action to create conditions that will help persuade refugees or displaced persons to return to their homes, such as improving security and rule of law, reinforcing respect for human rights, creating jobs, and more.

Like its post-conflict cousin, preventive peace building is especially useful in internal conflicts and can involve a wide variety of activities in the institutional, economic, and social fields. These activities usually have an intrinsic value of their own because of the contribution they make to democratization, respect for human rights, and economic and social development. What defines them as peace building activities is that, in addition, they have the political value of reducing the risk of the outbreak of a new conflict or the recrudescence of an old one.

The UN should, ideally, have the clinical capacity to prescribe the correct treatment for the condition diagnosed. To fulfill this condition, the Secretary-General needs to be able to assess both the factors that have created the risk of conflict and the likely impact on them of the various preventive treatments that are available. Making those judgments in an interstate situation is easier than in an internal one. In the first case, much can be learned from consultation with the states concerned, and with their neighbors, friends, and allies. In the second, the crisis is often due to ethnic or economic and social issues of an entirely internal nature and of great political sensitivity, and the potential protagonists may include non-state entities of questioned legitimacy and with shadowy chains of command. If in such circumstances the Secretary-General probes for the information needed to identify the right treatment, he can find himself accused of professional misconduct by infringing the sovereignty of the country concerned.

Another potential source of difficulty for the Secretary-General at this stage of the process is the need for triage. His analysis of the symptoms may lead him to conclude that there is no preventive action that the UN can usefully take. This could be because he judges that, contrary to the general impression, conflict is not actually imminent and that what is being observed is posturing or shadow-boxing rather than serious preparations for war. Or he may judge that there is no effective treatment that would be accepted by the parties, or even that there is no effective treatment at all.

Sometimes the situation is so threatening that the UN's efforts should be concentrated on stabilizing the patient and that, for the moment, the modalities for longer-term treatment become a matter of second priority. Unless the patients take their physician's advice seriously, most physicians would turn elsewhere. In internal conflicts, sovereignty is an added complication, and the Secretary-General has to proceed with great delicacy and finesse if he is to succeed in persuading both patients to consult the doctor and take the medicine he prescribes.

The salient fact that emerges from this analysis is that the Secretary-General's ability to take effective preventive action depends most critically on the political will of the parties to the potential conflict. In international politics, as in human medicine, the physician cannot impose treatment that the patient is not prepared to accept. Important improvements have been made in the Secretary-General's capacity to diagnose and prescribe. Failure to take effective prevention action is, in any case, only rarely due to lack of early warning; the symptoms are usually there for all to see. What is too often lacking at present is a predisposition by the parties to accept third party assistance in resolving their dispute.

Once a course of therapy has been defined and agreed upon by all concerned, decisions have to be taken on the modalities for its application. There is no fixed pattern. Specific modalities have to be worked out for each case. The Secretary-General's role can take many different forms. He can do the work himself, directly or through his Secretariat. He can refer the patients to specialists, such as the agencies of the UN system, regional organizations, individual Member States, or NGOs, and work with them to apply the therapy. He can coordinate the work of others or simply provide them with political and moral support.

Such public manifestations of the Secretary-General's concern can sometimes have a useful therapeutic effect. But more often he will prefer to provide his good offices quietly, especially where the looming conflict is an internal one. Quite apart from sovereignty-related sensitivities, it is easier for parties to make concessions when it is not publically known that they are being urged to do so by the Secretary-General of the UN who can guarantee little or nothing in return. As already mentioned, preventive diplomacy is usually best done behind closed doors, which can make difficulties for the Secretary-General if the world is clamoring for the UN to do something but he knows that to reveal what he is actually doing would impair his chances of success, as well as being the diplomatic equivalent of violating the Hippocratic oath.

Peace building is even more complicated. It can require a wide range and variety of actions not all of which will fall under the direct executive responsibility of the Secretary-General. His functions in his context are essentially those of a general medical practitioner. He can diagnose the patients' condition and advise them that certain general measures of a political, economic, or social nature will help reduce the risk of conflict. He must persuade the specialists to apply the therapy that he has prescribed and the patients have accepted. The best way of doing this, of course, is to associate the specialists with the earlier consultations and make them a part of the diplomatic process through which the parties are brought to accept the desirability of preventive action and the nature it should take.

There are no guaranteed vaccinations to prevent conflicts from starting and no miracle cures to end them once they have started. The best prevention is for the region or country concerned to follow a strict and healthy regimen of democratization, human rights, equitable development, confidence building measures, and respect for international law, while eschewing indulgence in such unhealthy practices as nationalism, fanaticism, demagoguery, excessive armament, and aggressive behavior. Most of the elements of such a regimen are prescribed in the UN Charter and in the corpus of international law.

The difficulties of prevention in the field of peace and security do not arise because the warning signs of conflict are more difficult to detect than those of human disease; on the contrary, they are usually more obvious. Nor is it that the therapies are less effective; many effective therapies have been devised over the years. The UN dispensary is well stocked and many experienced consultants and specialists are on call.

The problem is with the patients, and with the friends and enemies of the patients. Human beings may be full of phobias and superstition about disease but they can usually be relied upon to respond fairly rationally to the diagnoses and prescriptions of their physicians. The same cannot, alas, be said of governments and other parties to political conflicts. Many general practitioners would have been tempted to retire in despair long ago if their advice had been disregarded by their patients as consistently as the advice of the UN is disregarded by those to whom it prescribes therapies to avert imminent conflict. But the Secretary-General of the UN cannot abandon his principal duty any more than a conscientious physician can abandon a difficult case. The Secretary-General's duty is to use all the means available to him, be they political, military, economic, social, or humanitarian, to help the peoples and governments of the UN to achieve the goal, emblazoned in the first paragraph of its Charter, of "saving succeeding generations from the scourge of war."

I should like to add complementary thoughts from two other contributors to the Preventive Diplomacy conference. Jan Eliasson, who later became the Deputy Secretary-General of the UN, was, as a speaker at the 1995 conference, the Secretary of State for Foreign Affairs of Sweden. As a direct result of his involvement he instituted an official government policy in his country that all diplomatic actions and decisions should be examined through the prism of preventive diplomacy.

Lord Owen drew the inspiration for his lecture from an eighteenth century physician's cautionary advice: "Beware of overly aggressive doctors." In international relations, Lord Owen noted that by understanding—and accepting—limitations, and by using persuasion rather than reflex aggression, one might be able to prevent, or at least limit, a conflict. Alternatively, trying to extricate oneself from an unwise involvement, as in recent decades for Western Powers in Iraq or Afghanistan, can prove very difficult indeed.

In our ever more dangerous world, in the throes of both inter- and intrastate conflicts, the need for a new approach in international relations, seems obvious. Preventive diplomacy should deal with—and even direct—where a nation can move towards peace rather than replaying where it has been in endless wars. That surely was our intention in promoting this option, and neither Boutros nor I ever abandoned that dream.

It is most fitting that the venue for this first anniversary Memorial lecture in honor of Boutros Boutros-Ghali is at the United Nations

Headquarters, where his tenure as Secretary-General is remembered fondly by those who continue the search for peace, and that this address is sponsored under the broad mandate of the office of the UN Alliance of Civilizations (UNAOC), led by our CIHC Director and IIHA Diplomat in Residence, the former PGA Nassir Al-Nasser.

I conclude by returning to the importance of ideas. For Boutros believed, passionately, that ideas cannot be extinguished by mere political power. Boutros Boutros-Ghali—the scholar and teacher, the bibliophile and archivist, at the end of a most remarkable career as an unvanquished servant of his fellow man—donated his personal books and papers to libraries so that future generations can study his approaches to alleviate suffering and end conflicts through diplomacy. And, as a final codicil to this Memorial, it is a joy to report that the Francophonie, with the support of the Ministries of Defense of France, Belgium, and Canada, has recently established a Boutros Boutros-Ghali Observatory for Preventive Diplomacy.

Kevin M. Cahill, M.D.
UN Headquarters, New York
March 20, 2017

Appendices

IDHA Faculty*

The remarkable faculty list for the IDHA courses reflects the generous community of international diplomats, relief workers, academics, and military experts who have made essential contributions to the multi-disciplinary profession of international humanitarian affairs. In order to keep our tuition costs at a minimum, almost all faculty members participate gratis, waiving their usual lecture fees.

IDHA Alumni*

The long list of IDHA alumni provides the names of the graduates, their country of origin, and their affiliations with organizations or agencies around the world. Many of the graduates of our other courses are listed elsewhere.

IDHA Venues (1997–2017)

Amman, Jordan
Barcelona, Spain
Cairo, Egypt
Dublin, Ireland
Geneva, Switzerland
Goa, India
Kathmandu, Nepal
Kuala Lumpur, Malaysia
Nairobi, Kenya
New York City, USA
Pretoria, South Africa
Vienna, Austria

*You can find the list of our Faculty and Alumni on our website: http://www.cihc.org

2017 Humanitarian Training Courses

Spring

February 5–March 3
International Diploma in Humanitarian Assistance (IDHA) 49—Kathmandu, Nepal

March 20–March 24
Humanitarian Negotiators Training Course (HNTC) 15—Barcelona, Spain

March 27–March 31
Humanitarian Logistics 7—Barcelona, Spain

April 3–April 7
Community Participation and Mobilization in Humanitarian Response 8—Barcelona, Spain

April 10–April 14
Forced Migration 7—Barcelona, Spain

April 24–April 28
Disaster Management Training Course (DMTC) 9—Vienna, Austria

May 1–May 5
Strategic Issues in Humanitarian Affairs 5—Vienna, Austria

May 17–20, 2017
Sistema Global de Asistencia Humanitaria: Crisis y Respuestas (conducted entirely in Spanish) in partnership with Javeriana University—Cali, Colombia

Summer

June 4–July 1
International Diploma in Humanitarian Assistance (IDHA) 50—New York, USA

July 6–July 10
Data and Innovation Management in Humanitarian Action—New York, USA

Fall

September 23–October 2
Mental Health in Complex Emergencies (MHCE) 13—Amman, Jordan

October 2–October 6
Education in Emergencies 4—Malta

October 2–October 6

Urban Disaster, Vulnerability, and Displacement: Humanitarian Challenges 2—Vienna, Austria

October 2–October 6

Human Rights in Humanitarian Crises 6—Vienna, Austria

October 9–October 13

Ethics of Humanitarian Assistance 6—Vienna, Austria

October 16–October 20

Accountability in Humanitarian Action 5—Vienna, Austria

October 23–October 27

Leadership and Management of Humanitarian Action 5—Vienna, Austria

November 5–December 1

International Diploma in Humanitarian Assistance (IDHA) 51—Vienna, Austria

The IIHA Resource Library

Humanitarian action requires a diverse set of skills and knowledge. Resources do not sit in any one body of literature, but across a multitude of disciplines and languages. More suited toward the modern student, the IIHA has developed a comprehensive resource library that has its foundations in electronic links. These links allow access to the fundamental principles, standards, Conventions, Treaties, Charters, guidelines, and basic reference handbooks that a humanitarian student might require for background information.

Visit the IIHA Resource Library at www.fordham.com/iiha.

Contributors

Brendan Cahill is the Executive Director of the IIHA at Fordham University and an Officer for the CIHC.

Cynthia Coffman has worked in humanitarian operations in Haiti, Africa, and the Middle East. She is currently a Field Coordinator in Irbid, Jordan.

Naomi Gikonyo is an Emergency Preparedness and Response Officer in the WFP Regional Office for Southern Africa.

Ferdinand von Habsburg-Lothringen has worked for 22 years with UN agencies and NGOs in South Sudan. Currently seconded by the Swiss Federal Department of Foreign Affairs, he is Senior Advisor to the South Sudan Council of Churches.

Larry Hollingworth, CBE, is Humanitarian Programs Director for the CIHC and Visiting Professor at Fordham University's IIHA. He has led all 50 IDHA courses, as well as our other specialized training programs.

Mark Honnoraty, OBE, is a retired Commander of the Royal Navy. He is currently pursuing a Bachelor's Degree in Politics and International Relations at the University of Kent.

Lynne Jones, M.D., OBE, is a child psychiatrist, with 20 years of experience in mental health program management in conflict or disaster areas. Her diaries have appeared in a number of medical journals and as audio clips on the BBC.

Anthony Land, Ph.D., has spent his entire professional life in the aid world. His 24-year career with UNHCR took him to posts in Europe, Asia, and Africa. He is now a Senior Fellow for the IIHA.

Mark Little and *Angela Jackson* are a married couple who have worked together as team leaders for AUSMAT. Both are clinical practitioners at the Cairns Hospital in Queensland, Australia.

Orsa Lumbroso is Managing Director and Board Member of the Fondazione Marco Besso in Rome, which has provided over 80 scholarships for IDHA participants.

Joe Lowry is a Senior Media and Communications Officer for IOM, based out of the regional office in Vienna. He previously worked as a Senior Media Officer for IFRC.

Jesper Lund is the Head of Field Coordination Support for UNOCHA in Geneva.

Roger Mburente works as a lay theologian in Switzerland. He was a child refugee in Burundi, and has been a tutor on a number of IDHA courses.

Alexis Premkumar S.J., is continuing his studies within the MIHA, and has lectured to several IDHA classes on his ordeal as a hostage in Afghanistan.

Luvini Ranasinghe recently worked as the Manager of the Global Engagement Initiative at the IFRC headquarters in Geneva. She is currently on maternity leave, and we wish her our very best.

Florian Razesberger has worked on human rights issues for various international organizations. Most recently, he headed the human rights work of an OSCE Special Monitoring Mission in Ukraine. He has been a teacher and tutor on many IDHA courses.

Argentina Szabados is a member of the CIHC Board of Directors, and is the IOM Regional Director for South-Eastern Europe, Eastern Europe, and Central Asia. Her son is an IDHA alumnus, and her daughter was a Course Administrator.

Terence Ward and *Idanna Pucci* are both writers. Ward's latest books are the Seven Acts of Mercy and Searching for Hassan; Pucci authored the classic The Epic of Life: The Balinese Journey of the Soul.

How to Support the CIHC

With your donation we provide courses, trainings, and symposia given in partnership with Fordham University, offer dozens of scholarships to students from the Global South, and conduct on-going research and publications to promote best practices in humanitarian affairs. Please consider a recurring gift.

To donate online, please go to http://www.cihc.org/support. The link will take you to our secure payment processor.

You can also mail your gift to the CIHC at:
850 Fifth Avenue, New York, NY 10065.

We also accept donations of airlines miles, investments, bequests, etc. Please contact us at mail@cihc.org or (212)-636-6294 to discuss.

About the Author

Kevin M. Cahill, M.D., is University Professor and Director of the Institute of International Humanitarian Affairs at Fordham University, and President of the Center for International Humanitarian Cooperation in New York City. He is also Professor of Clinical Tropical Medicine and Molecular Parasitology at New York University, and Director of the Tropical Disease Center of Lenox Hill Hospital. He currently acts as Senior Advisor on Academic Affairs for the United Nations Alliance of Civilizations, and has served as Chief Advisor on Humanitarian and Public Health Issues for three Presidents of the United Nations General Assembly. His career in tropical medicine and humanitarian operations began in Calcutta in 1959; he has carried out medical, relief and epidemiologic research in 70 countries in Africa, Latin America, and Asia. He has written or edited 33 books, translated into many languages, and more than 200 articles in peer-reviewed journals on subjects ranging from tropical diseases to humanitarian and foreign affairs, Irish literature, and public health. He holds numerous Honorary Fellowships and distinguished awards from foreign governments, and has received dozens of Honorary Doctorates from universities around the world.